# A History of Jesuit Missions in Japan

In the aftermath of the religious crisis triggered by the Protestant Reformation, the Catholic Church set out to conquer faithful in new territories. The first missionaries to arrive in Japan were the Jesuits who were forced to adopt a different type of evangelization, with a bottom-up rather than a top-down approach. This volume shows that Japan turned out to be a land of experimentation and development of a global Catholicism, as well as an unprecedented laboratory of encounter between political, scientific and religious cultures in the age of the first globalization. It analyzes the different conversion strategies developed by the Jesuit fathers toward various groups, including samurai, Buddhist bonzes and Japanese peasants. A key step was the appropriation of sacred space by the missionaries: first in a violent way with the construction of large crosses and the destruction of temples, pagodas and pagan idols, then through strategies more flexible and accommodating of replacing pre-existing cultural practices. To be attractive, the Jesuit fathers had to compromise with local culture and spirituality, but they were also forced, in some way, to simplify and modify their very way of understanding and living Christianity. This book also reflects on the reasons for the failure of this ambitious Catholic conversion project: the hostility of the Japanese ruling class, the irreducibility of a different culture and spirituality, but also, if not above all, the rise of internal rivalries in Catholicism between Jesuits, Franciscans and Dominicans. This book marks a significant contribution to the literature on the history of the Jesuits, Catholic missions and Christianity in Japan.

**Guillaume Alonge** is Assistant Professor at the University of Turin, Italy.

# Young Feltrinelli Prize in the Moral Sciences

*Roberto Antonelli, President, Class of Moral Sciences,
Accademia Nazionale dei Lincei*

*Alberto Quadrio Curzio, President Emeritus, Accademia Nazionale dei Lincei*

*Alessandro Roncaglia, Joint Academic Administrator, Accademia Nazionale dei Lincei*

The Accademia Nazionale dei Lincei, founded in 1603, is one of the oldest academies in the world. Since 2018 it has assigned four "Young Antonio Feltrinelli Prizes" every two years, directed to Italian researchers in the fields of moral sciences and humanities who are less than 40 years old. Each winner is then requested to write a book-length essay on their research and/or the perspectives of research in their field, directed to the general public. The Routledge Young Feltrinelli Prize in the Moral Sciences series thus includes high-quality essays by top young researchers, providing thoroughly readable contributions to different research fields. With this initiative, Accademia dei Lincei not only gives a remarkable grant to the winners of the prize in order to support their research activity, but also contributes to the international diffusion of the research of eminent young Italian scholars.

**Pliny the Elder and the Matter of Memory**
An Encyclopaedic Workshop
*Anna Anguissola*

**Memory and Narrative at the origins of the Novel**
Three studies, from Chrétien de Troyes to Proust
*Lorenzo Mainini*

**Ancient Sacred Sites in the Gulf of Naples**
The Sanctuary of Athena at Punta Campanella
*Luca Di Franco*

**A History of Jesuit Missions in Japan**
Evangelization, Miracles and Martyrdom, 1549–1614
*Guillaume Alonge*

For more information about this series, please visit: www.routledge.com/Young-Feltrinelli-Prize-in-the-Moral-Sciences/book-series/YFP

# A History of Jesuit Missions in Japan
Evangelization, Miracles and Martyrdom, 1549–1614

**Guillaume Alonge**

LONDON AND NEW YORK

First published 2024
by Routledge
4 Park Square, Milton Park, Abingdon, Oxon OX14 4RN

and by Routledge
605 Third Avenue, New York, NY 10158

*Routledge is an imprint of the Taylor & Francis Group, an informa business*

© 2024 Guillaume Alonge

The right of Guillaume Alonge to be identified as author of this work has been asserted in accordance with sections 77 and 78 of the Copyright, Designs and Patents Act 1988.

All rights reserved. No part of this book may be reprinted or reproduced or utilised in any form or by any electronic, mechanical, or other means, now known or hereafter invented, including photocopying and recording, or in any information storage or retrieval system, without permission in writing from the publishers.

*Trademark notice*: Product or corporate names may be trademarks or registered trademarks, and are used only for identification and explanation without intent to infringe.

*British Library Cataloguing-in-Publication Data*
A catalogue record for this book is available from the British Library

ISBN: 9781032229775 (hbk)
ISBN: 9781032229782 (pbk)
ISBN: 9781003275008 (ebk)

DOI: 10.4324/9781003275008

Typeset in Times New Roman
by codeMantra

To Zeno, my little samurai

# Contents

|   |   |   |
|---|---|---|
| *Acknowledgments* | | ix |
| *Translator* | | xi |
| **Introduction** | | 1 |
| 1 | **Preaching a foreign God** | 11 |
| | Missionary violence  11 | |
| | Christ's samurai  13 | |
| | From persecutions to martyrdom  17 | |
| 2 | **Planting crosses** | 24 |
| | The conquest of sacred space  24 | |
| | Symbol of a suffering God  32 | |
| 3 | **The miraculous tree** | 47 |
| | The cross in the trunk  50 | |
| | Christianizing ancient cults  54 | |
| 4 | **The wood of martyrdom** | 65 |
| | Crosses of blood  65 | |
| | The Japanese roses of Nagasaki  70 | |
| 5 | **The Pope's samurai: Takayama Ukon** | 81 |
| | A living saint  81 | |
| | A martyr without martyrdom  88 | |
| | The post-mortem career: from failures to the altars  93 | |
| *Index nominum* | | 105 |

# Acknowledgments

Allow me to thank the Accademia Nazionale dei Lincei, which has offered me the opportunity to publish my work in this series. A feeling of gratitude also goes to those who, in recent years, have helped me enter the world of the Jesuit missions, have re-read or discussed parts of the manuscript. Among the many, allow me to mention Pierre-Antoine Fabre, whose Parisian seminars remain an inexhaustible source of stimuli, Natale Spineto, Massimo Firpo, Elena Bonora and Lucia Felici. A separate thought goes to Francesca who has made me discover Japan over the years.

# Translator

Stash Luczkiw is a translator of poetry, fiction and non-fiction from Italian to English.

# Introduction

The history of the Jesuit missions in Japan between the sixteenth and seventeenth centuries has interested scholars for many decades, and there are now numerous monographs and editions of sources published on the subject, all the more so after the general turning point in recent historiography. This little book certainly does not have the ambition to exhaust such a vast topic studied all over the world by researchers from the most disparate academic and linguistic contexts. Rather, the following pages are intended to be a story, among the many that can be imagined, of the Jesuit missions in Japan, starting from a point of view which obviously has to do with the abilities and limitations of the writer. It is a story that focuses on the gaze of the missionaries, because it is mostly based on the particularly rich and abundant sources left by the Jesuits over the centuries. A study therefore of the gaze of those men who came from the other side of the world to spread the message of the Gospel inserted into the Japanese reality, observing its inhabitants, cults, customs and habits, but also its food, drinks, landscapes and cities. A gaze destined to evolve over the decades, as exchanges with Japanese culture intensified, to transform and adapt, even at the cost of a thousand contradictions, compromises and misunderstandings. What interested this writer was certainly the Japanese reality itself, but also, if not above all, how it was caught by the eyes and ambitions of the missionaries, those special travelers who with their observations tell us what they understood of the Land of the Rising Sun; but at the same time, they tell us a lot about themselves, about their mentality, the horizon and vision of the sixteenth- and seventeenth-century European.[1] In the first age of globalization, the cultural identity of Europe was also forged in contact with realities that escaped its political, economic and religious control, as was the case of Japan during the period of the daimyos and samurai,[2] only open to trade with the monarchies and culture of Catholic Europe for a few decades.[3]

In accompanying the Jesuit priests in their discovery of the Land of the Rising Sun, it was decided to favor some thematic axes, some problematic nodes, which better than others allow us to enter the imagination of men and women of the early modern age, and which more clearly restore the sense of the missionary adventure at that time of globalization occurring under the

Iberian monarchies.[4] The first to "discover" Japan were Portuguese merchants in search of profit,[5] but almost immediately after them came men of God, soldiers of Christ, from the shores of the Mediterranean, from distant Europe ravaged by frightening and bloody religious conflicts, and whose identity owed much to the spiritual climate of the stark confrontation between Catholics and Protestants in which they had grown up.[6] The Society of Jesus, founded by Ignatius of Loyola, soon emerged as one of the Roman Church's most effective responses to the challenge launched by Martin Luther and the other great reformers. It was therefore in a logic of confrontation and competition, sometimes even violent – in which the souls of the faithful had suddenly become, after centuries, truly contestable – that the first Jesuits found themselves operating, determined to bring back into the fold of Roman orthodoxy those men and women seduced by the ideas of the Reformation. Conceived and structured as a real militia at the service of the papacy, the new order launched itself in search of souls to save in lands very distant from the heart of Roman Catholicism. Its members went where scarcely any Christian preachers had reached: India, South-East Asia, the Philippines, China, up to Japan, the Land of the Rising Sun, that "Cipangu" which Marco Polo had fantasized about in his *Milione*,[7] as yet untrodden by European feet. The effects of those transoceanic journeys were not limited to the religious sphere; they had significant repercussions in other areas, from politics to cartography to the diffusion of scientific, medical and architectural knowledge.[8]

Unlike other parts of the globe reached by Catholic missionaries, Japan was particular in that it was in no way subject to the military and political expansion of European powers, and still hardly involved in global trade. The geopolitical conditions had obvious repercussions on the penetration capacity of the Christian faith, which could not make use of force for converting the inhabitants of the archipelago. This does not mean that for the first decades the Jesuit missionaries did not give up their combative approach, entirely in line with the evangelization strategies experimented in Europe, the Americas and the rest of Asia. Playing on the contradictions and rivalries within the Japanese religious landscape, where Shinto, Buddhist and other religious sects had coexisted for centuries, they were able to ensure room for maneuver and obtain the protection of powerful feudal lords. Their proposal thus remained that of appropriating the public space by organizing disputes and debates with exponents of rival religions, exactly on the model of what they did in Europe with Protestant preachers. The missionaries sought to unmask the idolatry of the Buddhist bonzes and emphasize their contradictions and hypocrisies, their vices and their abuses. They were convinced that in this way they could ensure the approval of the Japanese faithful in search of an authentic faith, which better responded to their anxieties and spiritual concerns.

The verbal violence that pervaded the religious debate of sixteenth-century Europe, ignited by disputes among monks, bishops, pastors and reformed preachers, reappeared in the middle of the Pacific Ocean, and this despite the difficulty for the missionaries to follow on words with deeds. In some cases, however, when they succeeded in converting the daimyos and samurai, the Jesuits were the first to incite the neophytes to destroy Buddhist temples, statues and idols and to demand the expulsion of the bonzes from their lands. As such, a logic of violent confrontation remained, as did a project to replace the ancient cults with a new religious presence thought to be exclusive and uncontestable. The first chapter focuses precisely on the attempt to monopolize the space of the word through disputes and sermons, always in a performative logic that aspired toward a transformation into concrete acts of the fiery words launched from the pulpit and in the squares of the archipelago's cities. The second chapter observes this same phenomenon from a spatial point of view, focusing on the symbols used by the missionaries to physically occupy the places where the Japanese faithful lived. If in other contexts – certainly in old Europe, in opposition to the Protestants – statues of the Virgin and of saints were mainly valued, in the Far East the Jesuits privileged the use of the cross.[9] More than any other symbol, it was the cross of Christ's passion that was planted atop mountains, in city squares, on the spires of churches, but also inscribed on clothing, shields, katanas, helmets and banners of Japanese Christians.

The third chapter deals with the same effort of spatial colonization of ancient Japan by the missionaries from the point of view of the conquest of the imaginary. That is, it proposes to study the mechanisms, elaborated by the fathers, of substitution and Christianization of some symbols and stories typical of the local tradition. Particular reference is made to the cult of the tree, widely developed first in Shintoism and later in Buddhism, and taken up by the Jesuits in a Christian logic. Toward the end of the sixteenth century, coinciding with the first anti-Christian persecutions, signs of the cross began to appear miraculously – according to the stories of the missionaries – able to relaunch the evangelization of those lands and to announce the imminent conversion of the entire archipelago to the law of the Gospel. However, the transition from sermons and large crosses to tree trunks also marked an obligatory change in paradigm and strategy on the part of the missionaries.

The Jesuits' emphasis on substituting the cross, or rather its concealment inside the tree, and their search for correspondences and overlaps with pre-existing local cults are by no means ahistorical attempts to grasp the immobile and universal structures of religious phenomenon, which always remain eminently historical facts, inscribed in time's duration and conditioned by its flow. On the contrary, they result from an analysis that aims to grasp the adaptation and accommodation strategies elaborated by the missionaries interested in emptying ancient religious forms from within, in order to fill them with a different content, albeit keeping to an apparently common framework, and therefore more easily usable by the natives. Well before the current specialists in the history of religions, the Jesuits had intuited that the chances of successfully converting an individual were much greater if that person were convinced they would keep a substantial part of their initial religious capital in the transition from the old faith to the new. A foreign religion – such as Christianity in sixteenth-century Japan, or in the Mediterranean during the first centuries of the Christian era – had greater hopes of spreading among the pagans if it succeeded in establishing a sort of cultural continuity with the cults that had preceded it.[10] The existence of such correspondences between ancient and new cults is therefore not the fruit of the historical imagination and indulgent gaze of the twenty-first century scholar, but emerges clearly from the Jesuit sources themselves. The correspondences form part of the missionaries' mental equipment, as demonstrated, for example, by their gathering of information, even before setting sail for Japan, about local cultic forms in search of similarities: on the one hand, to understand if there had been in the past a subsequently forgotten Christian presence in the archipelago; and on the other, above all, to elaborate persuasive strategies of insertion and replacement.

The *accomodatio* method imposed itself, not without difficulty, in the great missionary laboratory that was Christian Japan. It came from the initiative of some Jesuits, as a response – which immediately proved to be adequate – to the changed attitude vis-à-vis their presence on the part of the Japanese political authorities at the tail end of the sixteenth century.[11] The new, more cautious and prudent way of proceeding, however, allowed the priests to remain on Japanese soil for many decades and to continue their proselytizing activity, even within the high aristocracy of the archipelago, despite the first edicts of expulsion. In addition to being an effective strategy developed for the conversion of the infidels and the survival of Christians in hostile lands, *accomodatio* was a distinctive, original and originary feature of a complex faith, with many facets, capable of adapting and shaping itself on the basis of the needs of the moment, and which, only at the price of many simplifications, could be brought *sic et simpliciter* into the bedrock of the most conservative Catholicism.[12]

But it should be specified that such a development in Japanese Christianity also depended on external factors. More prosaically, it depended on the reality of the mission in the land of the samurai and bonzes, since the missionaries' penury, about which the Jesuits never stopped complaining in their letters to Rome, did not allow them to adequately occupy the vast archipelago and ensure the appropriate pastoral and sacramental coverage for the numerous faithful converts. So physical persons were replaced by printed books and sacred objects,[13] especially crosses, through which those new Christians could learn to establish a direct, unmediated relationship with the God of Abraham. It also depended on the peculiarity of Japanese culture, which for centuries had been a sort of "alembic" – to use the beautiful image of Claude

Lévi-Strauss – capable of acting as a filter, of "distilling a rare, more subtle essence compared to those that had landed there, taken away by the currents of history," of "alternating borrowings and syntheses, syncretism and originality," without ever losing its specificity in the reworking of influences from outside.[14]

The protagonists of the second phase of soft evangelization were above all Italian missionaries, men like Alessandro Valignano and Organtino Gnecchi Soldo, who, not surprisingly, in their letters sent to Rome repeatedly invoked the desire to "especially see Italians arriving in this Japan whose natures get on well with the Japanese."[15] As has been observed, the religious culture in which those Jesuits from Italy had grown up and developed must have greatly influenced their flexible way of thinking about others, and the Nicodemitic attitude with which they faced persecution.[16] It is not surprising in this sense that the *accomodatio* approach was elaborated in Japan by Alessandro Valignano from Abruzzo and carried forward in other contexts as well – giving rise to similar controversies within the mission – by other Italians, such as Roberto de' Nobili in India[17] and Matteo Ricci in China.[18] Alongside cultural differences, the political dimension weighed heavily. Compared to the missionaries from the Iberian Peninsula, the Italians were less directly subject and accountable to the temporal dominance of Spain and Portugal's sovereigns. As such, they were exempt from double loyalty – to the pope and the king – and could therefore enjoy greater autonomy and freedom of action on a purely political level.

The fourth and fifth chapters deal with the last phase of the Christian presence in the Land of the Rising Sun, which corresponded to the decline of the Jesuit dream of Christianizing the archipelago peacefully. From promised land of evangelization on a global scale, Japan became a negative model of a society rejecting the truths of the Gospel, dominated by heinous persecutors thirsty for Christian blood. Thus was born the stereotypical image of Japan as a land of martyrs, where missionaries – but also local converts – suffered the worst tortures at the hands of the shogun's ruthless samurai. Through a myriad of printed texts, chronicles, plays and letters from the Far East, translated into various languages, but also of sermons and pictorial representations, this image spread and imposed itself on the imagination of the European faithful, who learned to measure themselves against the trials of those living saints of their time and model their daily faith on their heroism.[19] Through the case of Blessed Takayama Ukon – a daimyo who died in exile in Manila in order not to betray the faith to which he had converted as a child along with his entire family – the existence of different models of holiness produced by the laboratory of Christian Japan is highlighted. There were not only blood martyrs but also martyrs in perseverance, men and women who lived a daily martyrdom, made up of persecutions, renunciations and deprivations, without ever experiencing violent massacres. This model of holiness – typical of the Jesuits, also in a logic of opposition to the other religious orders – soon fell into disgrace both in Rome and in missionary letters and stories, because it was not very functional with respect to the image of the triumphant and combative Church of the Counter-Reformation. Rather, it was a model that corresponded better to what had been the spirit and historical project of the archipelago's evangelization as elaborated by the Society, and which survived for centuries in the hearts and prayers of the faithful, despite repeated failures in the race to sanctify their best representative. The case of Ukon demonstrates once again the vitality and originality of the missionary proposal, which was able to go beyond, and in some ways anticipate, the orientation of the Roman Church. Only after many centuries would he be accepted, moreover not without the inevitable processes of sugar-coating, to sanctify an indigenous candidate – a layman who was not just a soldier of Christ with a cross around his neck but a warrior holding the katana sword until his last days.

Analyzing the Jesuit presence in the Land of the Rising Sun allows for the recognition of greater complexity in the problematic nature of their missionary identity. The most modern aspects of their work are sometimes excessively highlighted in their approach to others, with the enhancement of their almost ethnographic curiosity and their remarkable ability to observe local cultures.[20] As if the fanatical Franciscan and Dominican missionaries, who in the Americas imposed the Christian faith with violence and without respect for the previous beliefs of the native peoples, could be countered by the moderate and tolerant efforts of the disciples of Ignatius and Francis Xavier, who preferred the gradualness of persuasion to domination, the slow conversion of the hearts and souls of individuals to superficial mass baptisms.

Of course, broadly speaking and at a superficial glance, the simplification seems to work, but the example of the first decades of Jesuit presence in Japan gives a more complex and fluid picture, inviting us to reconsider the alleged Jesuit exception.[21] In fact, it clearly shows that there were many ways of being a Jesuit missionary in pagan lands. Even the members of the Society – especially the Spanish and the Portuguese, including the "Apostle of the Indies" Francis Xavier – were children of the Church of the Counter-Reformation, which arose in opposition and in response to the Lutheran revolt, and was therefore accustomed to showing their most fanatical and intolerant face, focusing their preaching on the element of controversy against Buddhist sects, inciting converts to destroy pagan temples and idols, and imposing the new faith with the use of violence and mass baptisms where they were politically permitted.[22] Even within the granite compactness of the Society, disagreements, fault lines, evolutions, conflicts, strategies and missionary styles can be glimpsed that are different if not diametrically opposite. The prevalence, starting from the end of the 1580s, of the *accomodatio* line – imposed by Valignano, albeit not without disputes, and strongly invoked by the powerful aristocratic Japanese converts, who did not well tolerate being treated as an inferior people forced to conform to European culture[23] – implied the distancing of the priests from political dealings,[24] greater prudence though not less effectiveness in the work of evangelization, and, finally, a new approach to local culture and mentality. Accommodating the Japanese, however, did not mean only learning to dress,[25] behave, speak and drink tea like them. More significantly, it involved – at least in some cases – a profound effort of knowledge and adaptation to their way of thinking, believing and to living the faith.[26] Proof of this is the recovery and Christianization, exceptional in many ways, of traditional cults and rites, such as that of the tree and sacred branches – which, moreover, demonstrates how the method of *accomodatio*, based on the appropriation of language and imagery of the so-called popular traditions, was addressed, in the intentions of the fathers, not only to the privileged social classes but also to the humblest and simplest strata of the population.[27]

Thus, the mission appears to us as a land of religious and cultural experimentation, a laboratory of variations and exceptions with respect to the Tridentine dictates, a space of freedom, of autonomy, and at the same time the locus of rediscovery of a Christianity considered primitive and authentic. Here, in this light, the Jesuit fathers on mission in the Land of the Rising Sun and in the rest of Asia – even if not all of them and not always – appear distant from the rigidities, behavior, and, more generally, from the mentality of the Church of the Counter-Reformation,[28] and capable, in all likelihood, of becoming flexible and influential models for other contexts of evangelization, through a truly global circulation of practices and methods.[29] Compared to a stereotyped vision of a missionary and conquering post-Tridentine Catholicism that was always the same, what emerges is a plurality of approaches, styles, and even internal conflicts within the Catholic world, which, in the test of evangelization on a global scale, presented itself as anything but compact and supportive.[30] A multiplicity of ways of being missionaries, which can even be found within the Society of Jesus itself, from which opposing strategies emerge for the conquest of souls and the expansion of Christianity outside Europe. The existence of such contradictions and internal clashes, before the hostility of daimyos, samurai and bonzes, must be traced back to the ultimate reasons for the bankruptcy of the ambitious Catholic project of conversion of the Empire of the Rising Sun.[31] From such a jagged picture emerges once again the complexity of Counter-Reformation Catholicism and all the difficulty of reducing to the Tridentine paradigm the overall orientation and identity of the Church during the centuries of the modern age.[32]

## Notes

1 Jacques Proust, *L'Europe au prisme du Japon. XVIe–XVIIIe siècle*, Paris, Albin Michel, 1997.
2 Eiko Ikegami, *The Taming of the Samurai. Honorific Individualism and the Making of Modern Japan*, Cambridge/London, Harvard University Press, 1997 (1995).

## 8 Introduction

3 Serge Gruzinsky, *L'Aigle et le Dragon. Démesure européenne et mondialisation a XVI<sup>e</sup> siècle*, Paris, Fayard, 2012, p. 412.
4 Serge Gruzinsky, *Les quatre parties du monde. Histoire d'une mondialisation*, Lonrai, Editions de La Martinière, 2004, pp. 430–35.
5 Sanjay Subrahmanyam, *The Portuguese Empire in Asia, 1500–1700*, Chichester-Malden, Wiley-Blackwell, 2012 (1993), pp. 107–13; *La découverte du Japon, 1543–1552. Premiers témoignages et premières cartes*, ed. Xavier de Castro, Paris, Chandeigne, 2017, pp. 119–239.
6 Jurgis Elisonas, *Christianity and the daimyo*, in John Whitney Hall (ed.), *The Cambridge History of Japan, vol. 4, Early Modern Japan*, Cambridge, Cambridge University Press, 1991, pp. 301–72.
7 Marco Polo, *Il libro di Marco Polo detto Milione. Nella versione trecentesca dell'"ottimo"*, Torino, Einaudi, 1954, pp. 171–75; Alvise Zorzi, *Vita di Marco Polo veneziano*, Milano, Rusconi, 1982, pp. 219–23.
8 Antonella Romano, *Impressions de Chine. L'Europe et l'englobement du monde (XVI<sup>e</sup>–XVII<sup>e</sup> siècle)*, Paris, Fayard, 2016, pp. 130–43.
9 On the cross as the Christian symbol par excellence cf. Ugo Fabietti, *Materia sacra. Corpi, oggetti, immagini, feticci nella pratica religiosa*, Milano, Raffaello Cortina Editore, 2014, pp. 42–46.
10 Rodney Stark, *Le città di Dio. Come il Cristianesimo ha conquistato l'impero romano*, Torino, Lindau, 2010 [2006], pp. 159–62.
11 M. Antoni J. Ucerler, *The Samurai and the Cross. The Jesuit Enterprise in Early Modern Japan*, Oxford/New York, Oxford University Press, 2022, pp. 95–117; Inès G. Županov, *Accomodation*, in *Dictionnaire des faits religieux*, ed. R. Azria and D. Hervieu-Leger, Paris, PUF, 2010, pp. 2–3; Id. in collaboration with Paolo Aranha, *Accommodation, Accommodement*, in Pierre Antoine Fabre, Benoist Pierre (éd.), *Les jésuites. Histoire et dictionnaire*, Paris, Bouquins éditions, 2022, pp. 427–30; Carla Tronu Montane, *The Jesuit Accommodation Method in 16th and 17th Century Japan*, in José Martínez Millán, Henar Pizarro Llorente, Esther Jiménez Pablo (ed.), *Los jesuitas. Religión, política y educación (siglos XVI–XVIII)*, Madrid, Universidad Pontificia Comillas, 2012, vol. 3, pp. 1617–41.
12 Guido Mongini, *Maschere dell'identità. Alle origini della Compagnia di Gesù*, Roma, Edizioni di storia e letteratura, 2016, pp. 193–98; Michela Catto, Guido Mongini, *Introduzione*, in Michela Catto, Guido Mongini, Silvia Mostaccio (ed.), *Evangelizzazione e Globalizzazione. Le missioni gesuitiche nell'età moderna tra storia e storiografia*, Roma, Società Editrice Dante Alighieri, 2010, pp. 4–15; Pierre Antoine Fabre, *La question missionnaire dans la Compagnie de Jésus*, in Fabre, Pierre (éd.), *Les jésuites. Histoire et dictionnaire*, cit., pp. 375–78.
13 Hélène Vu Thanh, *Devenir Japonais. La mission jésuite au Japon. 1549–1614*, Paris, Presses de l'Université Paris-Sorbonne, 2016, pp. 190–200.
14 Claude Lévi-Strauss, *L'autre Face de la lune. Ecrits sur le Japon*, Paris, Seuil, 2011, p. 31.
15 Organtino Gnecchi to Everard Mercurian, Meac, Oct. 15, 1577, in ARSI, *Jap.sin.*, 8, I, f. 179v; almost ten years later Organtino insisted on the request to send Italian Jesuits: «Et perché vediamo questi star in molta propinqua disposizione sarà contenta V. P.tà fra li operarii che ci ha da mandare, scegliere alcuni di molte buone parti per governare questa gente del Giappone, perché conforme ai buoni talenti de li operarii si va augmentando, e conservando la conversione; *tra li quali potriano essere buon numero di italiani, poiché si confanno molto con la nature dei giapponi*, e pare che tali si potriano mandar di maniera che non siano impediti da i superiori delle Indie» (Miyako, 15 February 1596; ARSI, *Jap. sin.* 12, II, ff. 362r–63r; italics mine).
16 Proust intuits the existence of an "Erasmian sensibility" as well as a specific Italian line within the order (Proust, *L'Europe au prisme du Japon*, cit., pp. 73–87; Id.,

La supercherie dévoilée. Une réfutation du catholicisme au Japon au XVIIe siècle, Paris, Chandeigne, 2013, pp. 34–67). On the link between *accomodatio*, Italian spirit and heresy cf. also Adriano Prosperi, *Il missionario*, in Rosario Villari (ed.), *L'uomo barocco*, Roma-Bari, Laterza, 1991, pp. 190–202.

17  Ines G. Županov, *Le repli du religieux. Les missionnaires jésuites du 17e siècle entre la théologie chrétienne et une éthique païenne*, in «Annales HSS», 1996, 6, pp. 1201–23; Margherita Trento, *The Theater of Accomodation: Strategies for Legitimizing the Christian Message in Madurai (c. 1610)*, in Pierre-Antoine Fabre, Flavio Rurale (ed.), *The Acquaviva Project: Claudio Acquaviva's Generalate (1581–1615) and the Emergence of Modern Catholicism*, Boston, Institute of Jesuit Sources, 2017, pp. 109–27.

18  Romano, *Impressions de Chine*, cit., pp. 113–43; Ronnie Po-chia Hsia, *La Controriforma. Il mondo del rinnovamento cattolico (1540–1770)*, Bologna, Il Mulino, 2009, pp. 271–79.

19  Hitomi Omata Rappo, *Des indes lointaines aux scènes des collèges. Les reflets des martyrs de la mission japonaise en Europe (XVIe–XVIIIe siècle)*, Münster, Aschendorff Verlag, 2020.

20  Fabre, *La question missionnaire dans la Compagnie de Jésus*, cit., pp. 322–27.

21  Among the Franciscan and Dominican missionaries themselves in the Americas, different styles contrasted (Hsia, *La Controriforma*, cit., pp. 241–56).

22  Nathalie Kouamé, *Le christianisme à l'épreuve du Japon médiéval, ou les vicissitudes de la première mondialisation (1549–1569)*, Paris, Editions Karthala, 2016, pp. 41–42; Vu Thanh, *Devenir Japonais*, cit., pp. 185–90.

23  As has been observed, the *accomodatio* method was used systematically only in Japan and China, while in other contexts, always in Asia such as India, the scarce consideration for the capabilities of the local population, as well as the different balances of power politically and militarily, pushed the Jesuit missionaries toward a more intransigent line. See Paolo Aranha, *Gerarchie razziali e adattamento culturale: la «Ipotesi Valignano»*, in Adolfo Tamburello, M. Antoni J. Ucerler, Marisa Di Russo (ed.), *Alessandro Valignano S.I. Uomo del Rinascimento: ponte tra Oriente e Occidente*, Roma, Institutum Historicum Societatis Iesu, 2008, pp. 77–96. On the role of converts in building a Catholic identity in Japan cf. Vu Thanh, *Devenir Japonais*, cit., pp. 18–20.

24  In this sense, the arrival of Valignano, who immediately had to deal with the opposing missionary strategies of the Portuguese Francisco Cabral, was decisive. See Adriano Prosperi, *Il missionario*, cit., pp. 189–90; Pedro Lage Reis Correia, *Violence, Identity and Conscience in the Context of the Japanese Catholic Missions (16th Century)*, in Vincenzo Lavenia, Stefania Pastore, Sabina Pavone, Chiara Petrolini (ed.), *Compel People to Come In. Violence and Catholic Conversion in the non-European World*, Roma, Viella, 2018, pp. 104–9.

25  Matteo Sanfilippo, *L'abito fa il missionario? Scelte di abbigliamento, strategie di adattamento e interventi romani nelle missioni «ad haereticos» e «ad infideles» tra XVI e XX secolo*, in «Mélanges de l'Ecole française de Rome. Italie et Méditerranée», 109, 1997, pp. 601–20.

26  The conclusions reached in her remarkable work on the Jesuit mission in Japan by Hélène Vu Thanh (Vu Thanh, *Devenir Japonais*, cit., pp. 14–20, 311–17, 381–86) are partly different.

27  For the Indian case cf. Trento, *The Theater of Accomodation*, cit., pp. 117–23.

28  Valignano's decision not to publish the Tridentine decrees in Japan is significant in this sense. See Alessandro Valignano, *Sumario de las cosas de Japon (1583)*, a cura di José Luis Alvarez-Taladriz, Tokyo, Sophia University, 1954, pp. 138–39.

29  There certainly existed a circulation of models of Japanese and Filipino Christianity across the Pacific toward Spanish and Portuguese America, not necessarily

10  *Introduction*

    filtered by the Roman center, as evidenced by the resumption of the same approach suggested by Valignano and Organtino Gnecchi by the Jesuits in seventeenth-century Paraguay. On the other hand, Imbruglia does not refer to this hypothesis. See Girolamo Imbruglia, *L'invenzione del Paraguay. Studio sull'idea di comunità tra Seicento e Settecento*, Napoli, Bibliopolis, 1983, pp. 70–71; Id., *The Jesuit Missions of Paraguay and a Cultural History of Utopia (1568–1789)*, Leiden-Boston, Brill 2017, pp. 71–73.

30  Even the management and control of missionary holiness, often linked to martyrdom, generated internal conflicts in the Catholic world (Giovanni Pizzorusso, *Il martirio* in odium fidei *dalla realtà missionaria alla burocrazia romana: note di ricerca sul protonotario apostolico di Propaganda fide (XVII secolo)*, in «Annali di scienze religiose», 12, 2019, pp. 188–97; Id., *Governare le missioni, conoscere il mondo nel XVII secolo: La Congregazione pontificia de Propaganda Fide*, Viterbo, Sette Città, 2018, pp. 46–53).

31  Ucerler, *The Samurai and the Cross*, cit., p. 20–25, 188–91.

32  Massimo Firpo, *Riforma cattolica e concilio di Trento. Storia o mito storiografico?*, Roma, Viella, 2022.

# 1 Preaching a foreign God

## Missionary violence

There is a substantial difference between the evangelizing work of Catholic missionaries in the Americas and in East Asia, particularly in China and Japan. If in the Americas the preaching of the new faith to the natives went hand in hand with the political and military conquest by the Iberian monarchies, in Asia the missionaries had to move in a situation absent any Western military presence.[1] With the exception of a few merchants, the only Europeans to land and reside permanently in Japan starting from 1549 – the year Francis Xavier landed on the southern coasts of the island of Kyushu – were exclusively men of God, who arrived in those very distant lands from the other part of the globe to spread a message that in many ways was culturally and socially revolutionary, but completely incomprehensible to the Japanese. The small number of Jesuits – it was, in fact, the order founded by Ignatius of Loyola that first landed in the Far East and monopolized the evangelization effort for a few decades[2] – and the lack of political support from the Spanish or Portuguese commanders, which was not lacking in other contexts, such as India,[3] placed them in the difficult situation of having to develop new and completely peaceful strategies to ensure the conversion of the infidels. The task must have appeared all the more difficult to those men, who were mostly subjects of the kings of Spain and Portugal. Their spiritual and missionary formation had taken place in the European context of the wars of religion, in which recourse to armed support from the political powers in order to spread and defend the true faith had somehow always been an obligatory element.

Once they landed on the southern coasts of the Japanese archipelago, the first Jesuits instead had to deal with a social and political reality unknown to them, over which they were unable to exercise almost any type of coercive influence. As such, for the first few years, there were no forced conversions, let alone mass baptisms. Rather, the Jesuits made prudent attempts to convert the Japanese they encountered one by one, with recourse to the art of persuasion, reasoning and rational demonstrations regarding the superiority of the Christian faith,[4] ignoring the complex Tridentine dogmas of Baroque Catholicism[5] and focusing on the reasonableness of the Christian creed rather than on the

DOI: 10.4324/9781003275008-2

authority of Scripture and tradition.[6] The preaching of the word then appeared to those strangers dressed in simple clothes as the only weapon to spread the revolutionary message of the Gospel among the infidels. Meek, peaceful and accommodating, their life of poverty, abstinence and helping the needy was a persuasive example. This is the image that the Jesuit sources give us of that first Catholic presence in the Far East. As had been the case for the first Christians under the Roman Empire, in order to convince men and women to embrace the faith of the Gospel it was necessary, at least initially, to focus on the exemplary nature of one's lifestyle rather than on the transmission of overly complex dogmas and doctrines.[7]

A century later, the historian of the order, Daniello Bartoli, would reflect in the first pages of his book dedicated precisely to the Japanese mission on the theme of the relationship between conversion and the use of violence, which had characterized the expansion of the Christian faith almost everywhere. For the specific Japanese context, driven by the observation that episodes of destruction of temples and statues occurred immediately after the transition to the new faith, Bartoli identified three types of, so to speak, legitimate use of force for the purposes of evangelization.[8] The first type descended from the teaching of Augustine who had invited the Christians of his time to "deny nothing to zeal and concede nothing to indiscretion, but remove the insults of idols from the honor of God, where doing so does not inflict reasonable injury to the idolaters." That is, the acts of iconoclasm toward symbols and objects of worship considered idolatrous appeared legitimate to Augustine, without however going so far as to justify recourse to the use of force against the pagan faithful, "over whom, as he had no jurisdiction to force them to change the law, so he didn't even have the power to steal the statues of their idols, neither by stealth nor violence, and smash them." But the case was quite different, Bartoli affirmed, of the converted kings and princes, whose fervor could go further than that of the missionaries. Especially since the "Japanese princes were immediate masters of what is within the borders of their states," it was therefore in their power to strip their idolatrous subjects of their possessions, condemn them to exile, and consequently not tolerate "any apparent vestment of idolatry."

The shift from a sacred area to a profane one made it possible to justify the expulsion of the infidels and the destruction of their temples also from a political point of view: the bonzes, "masters and keepers of idolatry," were in fact also perceived as threats to the social order, scoundrels and seditious people ready to rebel against their lord, capable of "overthrowing kings and inciting neighboring peoples to take up arms and attack Christians" in order to regain lost benefits and honors. Bartoli thus distinguished between what was permitted to missionaries, peaceful men of God who tended to be extraneous to acts of violence, except toward sacred pagan objects left without owners, and the legitimate intervention, even violent, of Japanese converts, eager to preserve their own power and the social and political balance in their own lands. However, he took care to add a third type of legitimization of recourse to sacred violence, which allowed the introduction of a supernatural intervention: "The ruin of the Temples could be brought about by a particular impression of the Spirit of God motivating his faithful; and where not, it could be attributed to ignorance, easily excusable in men of great fervor and, if novices in the faith, much more in the ecclesiastical laws of positive reason."

Going through the letters sent from the Far East by the priests and the stories of the missions written subsequently, it clearly emerges that the episodes of violent destruction of Buddhist temples and statues, but also the occurrence of real armed clashes between new converts and bonzes, were anything but occasional.[9] Systematically, the passage of a fief to the Christian faith after the conversion of its lord, closely followed by all his subjects, involved the expulsion of the supporters of the ancient idols, the eradication, even material, of the ancient cult, soon replaced – as we will see in the next chapter – by the appearance of new symbols such as the cross and the construction of sacred Christian buildings. The missionaries were always prudent and careful in describing such acts of brutality as foreign to their will, and simply the fruit of the uncontrollable fervor of the converts. On some occasions, however, they did not fail to emphasize how the violence perpetrated was a just punishment desired from on high and guided by the Holy Spirit against the enemies of the Catholic faith. In some way it was therefore a legitimate, just and justifiable violence even if not expressly commissioned by the priests. So the amazed reaction of the Japanese lord Toyotomi Hideyoshi should come as no surprise: in 1587, on the occasion of the publication of the first anti-Christian announcement, he sent an emissary to the vice-provincial of the Society, Father Gaspar Coelho – at least according to Jesuit sources – to ask him about the unscrupulous (in his eyes) evangelization policy implemented by the Christians. "He wanted to know why the priests went with such thirst to incite men to become Christians, even by force, and why they ruined and destroyed the temples [...] persecuting the bonzes who did not agree with them."[10] In a multi-religious context such as Japan, where various Buddhist sects and previous Shinto cults had coexisted peacefully for centuries, the claim to impose a single faith at the expense of other devotions must have seemed incomprehensible.

## Christ's samurai

Clearly, the perception of the Jesuits' missionary activity was very different from what they themselves recounted in their self-exculpatory letters. Although in a subordinate position with respect to the local political authorities, in the first decades of their presence in Japan the strategy implemented by the missionaries – mostly of Iberian origin – proved to be aggressive and intolerant toward Buddhism and Shintoism. The influence exerted on Portuguese merchants allowed the Jesuits to direct their ships toward one port rather than another on the Japanese coasts. Lacking military power, they played on the economic element to condition the religious policy of the Japanese daimyos. The arrival of Western boats on their coasts and the beginning of commercial relations with China through Portuguese mediation were lucrative objectives for the lords of the archipelago, who did not hesitate to bow to the requests of the missionaries in order to guarantee for themselves that profitable trade.[11] Over the years, the Christian presence, especially on the island of Kyushu, grew stronger thanks to the conversion or benevolence of several daimyos and samurai: conversions mostly linked to economic conveniences, but which offered the Jesuits solid political and even military support. For some of them, in particular the Portuguese superior of the Japanese mission, Francisco Cabral, the perspective changed substantially. After a few decades of effective difficulty and subordination to political power, Christians could now count on the support of powerful warriors, willing to resort to arms to spread the new faith. In the always turbulent scenario of civil war that had characterized the Japanese archipelago for decades, the religious theme also played a role in the various feudal potentates' attempts at expansion. The ambitious goal of the Jesuits became that of uniting the Christian daimyos under a single Crusader flag to force the remaining Buddhist lords to convert by force of arms.

The fear of an alliance between the Christian daimyos of the South and the sensational about-face of Hideyoshi in 1587 have been linked, and not without foundation.[12] Up to then, and in the wake of the conduct of his predecessor, Oda Nobunaga, Hideyoshi had tolerated the proselytism of the Jesuits, with whom he had maintained cordial relations.[13] However, during the expedition in Kyushu, also destined to aggregate those lands to the rest of Japan by now unified under his authority,[14] he realized the worrying influence exercised by those foreign priests on many warriors, their capacity to mobilize militarily, as well as the risk that, for religious reasons, a part of the archipelago could one day rebel against his power and facilitate an external attack by the Spanish monarchy.[15] Such fears were probably unfounded, as demonstrated by the sudden conversions of many of those daimyos to the ancient faith in the aftermath of the anti-Christian edict of 1587, but sufficient to bring about a long-lasting change in relations between Japanese authorities and European missionaries.[16]

Up to that point, in fact, there had been no shortage of episodes of the establishment of Crusader samurai armies, as attested in particular by the case of the converted daimyo Takayama Ukon.[17] In his lands, the Japanese lord, destined centuries later to access the glory of the altars as blessed by the pope, had the Jesuits preach and convert most of his subjects. At the time of participating in the expedition to Kyushu commissioned by Hideyoshi, he invited his warriors to inscribe crosses and "insignia of the mystery of the passion" on their banners in order to distinguish themselves in the great army of samurai. And in fact, at the moment of reunification with the troops of the other daimyos, the missionary fathers were amazed at the sight of those Crusader knights among the many pagans: "And what comforted us most was to see the Christians, who within the same company and squadrons of Gentiles went armed with crosses both in their helmets and in their flags; and thus armed they came to our church in passing to make orations."[18] A few weeks later, once the conquest of Kyushu was completed, Ukon himself fell out of favor with Hideyoshi precisely because of his refusal to abandon the Christian faith. He was deprived of all his lands and titles, and sentenced to a life of exile, which culminated in 1614, when he embarked for Manila with the last missionaries.[19]

By contrast, another powerful Christian lord, Konishi Yukinaga – in Jesuit sources he is known by the Christian name of Agostinho – despite his open adherence to the Christian faith, remained in vogue for all the years Hideyoshi was in power, being one of his primary vassals and advisers.[20] Precisely because of the esteem in which he was held by the unifier of the archipelago, he was entrusted with the ambitious Korean expedition in the 1590s, initially intended to culminate in the subsequent conquest of China, but which instead ended in a military catastrophe.[21] Upon Hideyoshi's death, Konishi led the Army of the West together with Ishida Mitsunari and the remnants of the Toyotomi clan in the decisive Battle of Sekigahara in 1600.[22] Instead, Tokugawa Ieyasu, ruler of the East and new undisputed master of the now reunified and pacified Japanese archipelago, prevailed. However, the case of Konishi demonstrates how, even decades after the beginning of anti-Christian persecutions, there remained room for maneuver, even at very high levels of the social hierarchy, for converts and supporters of the God of Abraham. These were men who did not hesitate to use their influence to protect and encourage the further diffusion of Christianity, especially in court circles, but who – notwithstanding Jesuit apologetics tending to clear away the most contradictory aspects of the Christian daimyos – did not cease being shrewd men of government and ferocious warriors.[23]

The ability of Christianity to make inroads among the Japanese aristocratic elite had very significant consequences to the extent that, through those new converts of high lineage, the Jesuits had access to political power, and consequently had at their disposal effective, even coercive, instruments of pressure on subjects not yet converted. An example of this is the story of the second son of the Bungo daimyo Ōtomo Yoshishige, also known as Sōrin. Destined for a religious career as a bonze, the young scion from an early age showed dissatisfaction with this fate. Instead, he approached the missionaries, and eventually his father accepted his conversion to the Christian faith with the name of Sebastiano. The conversion, however, triggered the process of a progressive social revaluation of that religion brought by the Barbarians who came from the sea, which until then had spread mostly among the humblest strata of society, and for this very reason had met with little interest among the aristocratic elite. Out of convenience or out of conviction, many other nobles followed Sebastiano on the road to Christianity,[24] espousing violent attitudes toward Buddhist places of worship, as recounted in great detail and not without a certain satisfaction by a Jesuit missionary in a letter from September 9, 1576:

> And on the same day of Christmas, having called all those Christian knights to him, he ordered them to put rosaries around their necks, as he

did, and with this noble squad he went on foot through the main streets of the city, and finding some pagodas he had them razed to the ground. And when I asked him why he was doing this, that it would be the cause of some tumult, and that perhaps the king would not hold him dear, he replied that he did it on purpose, so that everyone would know that he was a Christian, and that even the next day he wanted to go by other roads and do the same. I now leave it up to your paternity to judge the jubilation of all Funai's Christianity, seeing the son of the Christian king with so many other respectable people, since up to that time the Christians had been so abject and so vile that they did not dare appear, partly for being few compared to so many Gentiles, partly because the said Christianity began in the hospital, where we cared for people who were lowly and sick with contagious diseases.[25]

The Jesuit abstains from condemning the violent and iconoclastic attitude of the new convert, and indeed seems to exalt his clear manifestation of Christian fervor. Moreover, the story of samurai who, as soon as they abandoned their idolatrous faith, give concrete proof of their spiritual breakthrough with the destruction of once-revered religious symbols reappears almost obsessively in missionary letters, to the point of constituting a sort of cliché. This must lead us to reflect on the fact that the lack of recourse to sacred violence on the part of the missionaries was a necessity in the first decades of their presence in the Far East rather than a real and proper choice. But once they achieved a certain ability to influence the political scenario in specific areas of the archipelago, the fathers did not hesitate to re-propose models of evangelization based on coercion and the destruction of Buddhist temples. The model of exporting the faith among the unbelievers remained the one inherited from the crusader culture of Spain's Reconquista against the Moors, and then relaunched by the Church of the Counter-Reformation from an anti-Protestant perspective.[26] Clear evidence of this is the establishment of Crusader samurai armies, the attempts of the Jesuits to favor a union of the various Christian princes of Kyushu, but also more concretely the foundation of a real Christian fortress city, Nagasaki, which in a few years went from a small fishing village to a city of 50,000 inhabitants and the capital of trade between the archipelago and the Asian continent through the mediation of Portuguese merchants.[27] But Nagasaki also became the capital of Japanese Christianity and the seat of the first diocese.[28] The very management of the city, on the basis of generous concessions from the local lord, was entrusted to the direct government of the Society of Jesus, so that "no idolater was tolerated there, except for a short passage."[29] And those missionaries who had come from afar to bring the message of the Gospel did not hesitate to participate in trade to secure the resources necessary to feed the expenses of the mission, but also to fortify the walls of the city and make it impregnable in the event of an increasingly probable assault by enemies of the faith.[30] In his *Sumario de las cosas de Japon* of 1583, Alessandro Valignano, in describing the Jesuit port, dwelt precisely on the defensive nature of its walls:

> This port of Nagasaki is very strong because it has a high point of land that extends so far into the sea that it is almost everywhere surrounded by sea, and on the part that continues with the land it is very fortified with its bulwarks and caves, and at the end of this point is our house, which is like a fortress, separated from the rest of the town.[31]

At the end of the century, when Japanese Christianity was reaching its apogee, thick clouds were beginning to gather over it: the time of glorious expansion would soon be replaced by that of persecutions. From a violence preached, and in some cases practiced in the name of faith, to a violence suffered.

## From persecutions to martyrdom

At the end of the sixteenth century, the repressive offensive of the Japanese authorities against the faith in the foreign God started from Nagasaki. In 1587 Hideyoshi had officially banned Christianity from the Land of the Rising Sun and forbade the priests to continue their proselytizing work, but then in fact tolerated their stay. In more cautious and less showy ways, following the indications of the skillful Valignano, the Jesuits had thus managed to enter the aristocratic circles of the Japanese archipelago, in particular among the women, soon compared by the missionaries in their writings to the matrons of ancient Rome who protected the new faith.[32] The depoliticization of Christianity – which in this new course renounced exercising too direct an influence on the internal political affairs of Japan, now almost completely unified – seemed to open up new room for maneuver and further diffusion, even in areas hitherto less affected by the missionary message, such as the northern regions of Honshu.

The arrival of other missionary orders, in particular the Franciscans and Dominicans, contributed to drastically changing the course of events and to imprinting a dramatic turning point on the history of the mission in Japan, which from the early 1590s arrived on the ships of Spanish merchants, well established in the neighboring Philippines and eager to establish trade relations with the country of samurai. Within a few years, a situation of competition arose between religious orders engaged in the effort to convert Japanese souls, a situation all the more unpleasant for the Jesuits, who had exercised a sort of monopoly over the archipelago for over 40 years. The attitude of the new arrivals, especially the Franciscans, proved to be destabilizing due to the balance painstakingly built over many decades by the Society of Jesus with the local authorities. On the one hand, it revealed to the Japanese the existence of many versions of Catholicism, by now no different in their eyes than the rivalry among Buddhist sects, thus discrediting one of the cornerstones on which their proselytizing activity was based: namely, the claim of coherence and unity of the Christian world. On the other hand, it re-proposed a particularly aggressive and imprudent approach to the methods of public preaching of the new faith, in clear violation of the ban imposed by Hideyoshi.

The quarrels between the Jesuits and the Franciscans, combined with the resumption of proselytism conducted without foresight, led the authorities to punish the Christians with a decisive strike: in January 1597, 6 Franciscans, 17 Japanese faithful of the same order, and 3 dōjuku (Japanese preachers) of the Society of Jesus were arrested in Kyoto. After having crossed half of Honshu, and having suffered torture and public humiliation, the 26 Christians were taken to Nagasaki, more precisely to Mount Tateyama in front of the city, where they were crucified on February 5, 1597. The dramatic epilogue marked a point of no return in the history of Japanese Christianity and inaugurated an era of persecutions and massacres. It affected missionaries of all orders without distinction, but above all the Japanese faithful converted to the foreign God. The violence that for years, at least in part, missionaries had been able to exercise directly – with iconoclastic words and deeds – and to instill in the converts against their former co-religionists, now assumed an opposite value: violence suffered, experienced on their own skin as evidence of an unshakable faith. Those men who came from all over Europe, who had trained for years in Jesuit colleges on the model of the martyrs of the early Church, were now called to put into practice, with the shedding of their own blood, a vocation to self-sacrifice long-invoked and somewhat desired.[33] Death on the cross, which for Japanese culture was a mark of infamy for thieves and criminals, assumed in the eyes of those Christians of the Land of the Rising Sun and their Western priests a completely different connotation: it was the culmination of a process of full identification with the Savior, the son of God who came to redeem all humanity with his sacrifice. And just as Christ with his death had started the conversion of the whole world – or so those first martyrs and their zealous hagiographers deluded themselves – their sacrifice on the crosses erected by Hideyoshi's samurai prefigured a radiant destiny of conversion of the entire archipelago. Moreover, Tertullian had taught them: "The blood of martyrs is a seed that generates new Christians." The continual evocation of the epic of the primitive Church, of those first communities of faithful persecuted by the Roman emperors, was in this sense fully functional to the attribution of a positive meaning to those dramatic events, because, as had happened centuries before, even now, confronted with new pagans and new tyrants, the Asian Christians of the sixteenth and seventeenth centuries should not lose faith in God's providential plan. Through their suffering the new global Church was being built, destined in spite of everything to triumph.

The intensification of the persecutions aroused different reactions in the various missionary orders: the Jesuits hesitated for a long time before embracing the prospect of exalting those courageous acts of testimony in the name of faith, and they pursued, for a few more years, the illusion that more cautious attitudes would allow them to re-establish peaceful relations with the authorities and to resume a prudent work of evangelization without the threat of death on the cross. Instead, the approach of the Franciscans turned out to be quite different, as they exalted martyrdom to an excess, made it a boast of their clear fidelity to the evangelical dictates, and proof of their different Christian identity compared to the less credible Jesuits, too compromised by the local culture. A ruthless struggle took place between Catholic missionary orders with regard to the memory of martyrdom – violence suffered and sought. Each referred to profoundly different conceptions of Christianity – indeed, competing and irreconcilable. From the very first days, the Franciscans launched a propaganda campaign based on the publication of numerous pamphlets in which the 26 Martyrs of Japan, in Nagasaki, and the miraculous events that followed were told in detail, causing hundreds of conversions to the new faith. The propaganda was addressed not only to a Japanese or European audience; the same texts were in fact published in Europe and also in the Americas, in Mexico City, attesting to the global scale of events.[34] Cycles of frescoes painted in churches and convents throughout the world also contributed to the project of exalting the Christian faith through the evocation of martyrdom. Particularly instructive is the fresco in the cathedral of Cuernavaca, dating back to the early seventeenth century, in which the faithful Mexicans could see reproduced in images the whole story of the martyrdom of the 26, from their arrest, to the long journey through central Japan, up to the Christological death on the cross.[35]

The history of the Christian presence in Japan in the sixteenth and seventeenth centuries reveals that the underlying logic of the so-called first globalization, an Iberian globalization, was based above all on the competitive dimension of the clash between cultures and civilizations, and only secondly did it become an occasion for meeting and discovery.[36] The Catholic world that came into contact with the immense and elusive physical and mental world outside of Europe was pervaded by internal tensions, reeling from decades of civil wars and the violence behind it. It was mostly religious violence, due to the split of Christian unity and the mortal struggle against the Muslim infidels as well as the Lutheran and Calvinist heretics. Outside its borders, that still-crusading Europe thus revived the mental mechanisms and practices based on identity and culture that were pervaded by an intolerant, repressive and inquisitorial mindset. What guided the missionaries – even the first Jesuits – was the conviction of having to bring the faith to the infidels by any means, even at the price of resorting to violence, a violence imagined, practiced and finally suffered. Yet the encounter/clash with the Other in those lands thousands of kilometers away from the European coasts and from the heart of Counter-Reformation Catholicism also became the laboratory for the development of more refined and subtle proselytizing strategies, based on a real attempt to understand and an openness to the novelty of encountering very distant cultures and conceptions, as demonstrated by the success of the *accomodatio* advocated by Valignano and the other Italian missionaries in the Far East. It was a strategy in many ways antithetical to what had been practiced up to then in the missions and destined to arouse insurmountable resistance within the Roman Catholic world itself. In the next chapter we will see how these more or less invasive strategies of penetration into the Japanese archipelago were articulated with different perspectives of occupation, appropriation or restructuring of public space.

## Notes

1 As has also been emphasized in the Paraguay missions, the Jesuits were able to avail themselves on the occasion of Spanish military support or that of the already Christian Indians to induce the most riotous to convert (Imbruglia, *L'invenzione del Paraguay*, cit., pp. 28–29, 75–78; Id., *The Jesuit Missions of Paraguay and a Cultural History of Utopia (1568–1789)*, cit., pp. 45–46, 56, 108; for a comparison between the two editions see Niccolò Guasti, *Alcune riflessioni sul libro di Girolamo Imbruglia,* The Jesuit Missions of Paraguay and a Cultural History of Utopia (1568–1789), *Leiden-Boston, Brill 2017*, in Guido Mongini (ed.), *Utopie e comunità religiose tra età moderna e contemporanea*, Alessandria, Edizioni dell'Orso, 2021, pp. 75–86.
2 On the Japanese mission see at least the most recent works of Ucerler, *The Samurai and the Cross.*, cit.; Vu Thanh, *Devenir Japonais*, cit.; Osami Takizawa, *La historia de los Jesuitas en Japon (siglos XVI–XVII)*, Alcalá de Henares, Universidad de Alcalá, 2010; Id., *Los jesuitas en el Japón de los samuráis (siglos XVI–XVII)*, Madrid, Digital Reasons, 2018.
3 Ines Županov, *Missionary Tropics. The Catholic Frontier in India (16th–17th Centuries)*, Ann Arbor, The University of Michigan Press, 2005.
4 Kouamé, *Le christianisme à l'épreuve du Japon médiéval*, cit.
5 Significantly among the not very numerous works translated and printed by the Jesuits in Japan are the *Introducción del Símbolo de la Fe and the Guia do peccador* by the Spanish Dominican Luís de Granada (Vu Thanh, *Devenir Japonais*, cit., pp. 194–99). On the Paulinism of Luís de Granada cf. Mongini, *Maschere dell'identità*, cit., pp. 176, 360–61, 374.
6 Proust, *L'Europe au prisme du Japon*, cit., pp. 34–52; Vu Thanh, *Devenir Japonais*, cit., pp. 208–9.
7 Stark, *Le città di Dio*, cit., pp. 16–21.
8 Daniello Bartoli, *Dell'Historia della Compagnia di Giesù. Il Giappone, seconda parte dell'Asia*, Roma, Ignatio de' Lazzeri, 1660, pp. 34–35 (also for subsequent citations). There is a modern but only partial edition of Bartoli's book on Japan: Id., *Asia. Istoria della Compagnia di Gesù*, ed. by Umberto Grassi and Elisa Frei, introduction by Adriano Prosperi, Torino, Einaudi, 2019.
9 For example, Bartoli praises the just punishment received by a bonze for setting fire to a Christian church: another infidel, mistaking him for a missionary, killed him (ivi, p. 27).
10 *Lettera annale del Giapone scritta al padre generale della Compagnia di Giesù alli xx di febraio M.D.LXXXVIII*, Roma, Appresso Francesco Zannetti, 1590, p. 56.

Preaching a foreign God   21

11  Charles R. Boxer, *The Christian Century in Japan, 1549–1650*, Manchester, Carcanet Press, 1993 (Cambridge 1951), pp. 145–49.
12  Lage Reis Correia, *Violence, Identity and Conscience in the Context of the Japanese Catholic Missions (16th Century)*, cit., pp. 106–10.
13  Ninomiya Hiroyuki, *Le Japon pré-moderne, 1573–1867*, Paris, CNRS Éditions, 2017, pp. 47–48.
14  Asao Naohiro, *The Sixteenth-Century Unification*, in *The Cambridge History of Japan, vol. 4, Early Modern Japan*, cit., pp. 40–95.
15  Mary Eilzabeth Berry, *Hideyoshi*, Cambridge-London, The Harvard University Press, 1982, pp. 87–93.
16  On the Christian daimyos cf. Michael Steichen, *Les daimyō chrétiens ou un siècle de l'histoire religieuse et politique du Japon, 1549–1650*, Hong Kong, Imprimerie de la société des missions étrangères, 1904.
17  See below, chap. 5.
18  "Et quello che a noi più confortava era vedere gli cristiani che dentro la medesima compagnia et squadroni de gentili andavano armati con croci assì negli elmi come nelle bandiere et così armati de passaggio venivano nella nostra chiesa a fare orationi" (Archivum Romanum Societatis Iesu, J 10, II, f. 279Bv: Prenestino to Claudio Acquaviva, Hirado, 1 October 1587).
19  Johannes Laures, *Takayama Ukon. A Critical Essay*, in «Monumenta Nipponica», 5 (1942), pp. 86–112; Id., *Takayama Ukon und die Anfänge der Kirche in Japan*, Münster, Aschendorsffsche, 1954.
20  Maria Grazia Petrucci, *In the Name of the Father, the Son and the Islands of the Gods. A Reappraisal of Konishi Ryusa, a Merchant, and of Konishi Yukinaga, a Christian Samurai, in Sixteenth-Century Japan*, A thesis submitted in partial filfilment of the requirements for the degree of master of arts in The Faculty of graduate studies (Asian Studies), Vancouver, The University of British Columbia, 2005.
21  Jurgis Elisonas, *The Inseparable Trinity: Japan's Relations with China and Korea*, in *The Cambridge History of Japan, vol. 4, Early Modern Japan*, cit., pp. 271–300.
22  Julien Peltier, *Sekigahara, la plus grande bataille de samouraïs*, Parigi, Passés composés, 2020.
23  The wife of a feudal lord of Konishi during the Korean War managed to convert a large part of her court, of which the Jesuit father Gregorio Fulvio has left us a beautiful fresco in a letter to the provost general Acquaviva, dated 15 February 1596: "[The wife] Governò con molta prudentia sua casa e sua gente che tiene 30 o più donne di servitio et era quella casa come monasterio; perché ogni giorno havia determinato tempo per l'oratione tre volte la mattina, e mezzo giorno e poco doppo, e la sera agiutando la sua gente facendo esame di conscientia e di poi lei dir le litanie e l'altre responder havendo in sua casa un altro molto ben accomodato a suoi predicare quasi ogni giorno voleva o dir messa e o dir cose spirituali, ed digiuni e discipline, e il giovedì santo ascosa molto e descognosciuta venne al sepulcro nella chiesa disciplinandose di sangue come di poi seppi, di modo che havia necessità. [...] In questa parte anco passava in un certo modo i termini. [...] Et havendogli suo marito mandate molte pezze di damasco e da altri drappi per suoi vestiti e per altre cose, li pare miglior mandare alla chiesa per far ornamenti che vestirsi lei" (Archivum Romanum Societatis Iesu, Jap. sin. 12, II, fol. f. 360*r*).
24  "Et perché in compagnia di don Sebastiano erano venuti alcuni cavallieri gentili, al tempo della Messa gli fece uscir di chiesa, ne sopportò che altri, che christiani vi rimanessero, et il giorno seguente disse alla chiara, che non voleva più in sua compagnia nessuno che non si risolvesse di pigliar la medesima fede. Là onde quasi tutti venivano a dimandare il battesimo" (*Lettere diverse dalle Indie orientali di nuovo venute; le quali narrano molte cose notabili del gran regno del Giappone*,

*negli anni. 74. 75. & 76, scritte dalli reverendi padri della compagnia di Giesù; et di portughese tradotte nel volgare italiano*, in Turino, 1579, pp. 52–53).

25 "Et l'istesso giorno di Natale, chiamati a sé tutti quei cavallieri christiani, ordinò loro che si ponessero i rosari al collo, com'egli faceva, et con questa nobile squadra se ne andò a piedi per le strade principali della città, et ritrovando alcuni pagodi gli faceva gittare a terra, et dicendogli io perché faceva questo, che sarebbe cagione di qualche tumulto, et che il re forse non l'havrebbe caro, mi rispose che lo faceva a posta, acciochè tutti sapessero come egli era christiano, et che anco il giorno dopo voleva andare per altre strade et fare l'istesso. Lascio hora giudicare a vostra paternità il giubilo di tutta quella christianità di Funai, vedendo il figliuolo del re christiano con tante altre persone di rispetto, poiché fino a quella hora i christiani erano stati sì abietti et sì vili, che non ardivano comparire, parte per essere pochi, rispetto a tanta quantità di gentili, parte perché la detta christianità cominciò nello spedale, del quale noi tenevamo la cura, da gente bassa et inferma di mali contagiosi" (Ivi, p. 53).

26 The conversion on the other hand, starting from the lords to get to the vassals, and the diffusion of the model of the lay brotherhoods are other examples of a medieval Christianity of Iberian origin imported into Japan according to Osami Takizawa, *La continuidad de la mentalidad medieval europea en la misión de Japón. En torno a la política de evangelización*, in «Hispania Sacra», LXII, 125 (2010), pp. 27–42.

27 On Nagasaki as a global city resulting from the encounter between different cultures, also from the planimetric and architectural point of view, see Cristina Castel-Branco, Guida Carvalho, *Luis Fróis: First Western Accounts of Japan's Gardens, Cities and Landscapes*, Singapore, Springer Nature Singapore, 2020, pp. 42–53 Reiner H. Hesselink, *The Dream of Christian Nagasaki: World Trade and the Clash of Cultures, 1560–1640*, Jefferson, McFarlan, 2016; Carla Tronu Montane, *Sacred Space and Ritual in Early Modern Japan: The Christian Community of Nagasaki (1569–1643)*, PhD Thesis, University of London, School of Oriental and African Studies, 2012.

28 Carla Tronu Montane, *The post-Tridentine Parish System in the Port of City of Nagasaki*, in Nadine Amsler, Andreea Badea, Bernard Heyberger, Christian Windler (ed.), *Catholic Missionaries in Early Modern Asia. Patterns of Localization*, New York, Routldege, 2020, pp. 82–95; Ead., *Sacred Space and Ritual in Early Modern Japan*, cit., pp. 162–201.

29 Bartoli, *Dell'Historia della Compagnia di Giesù. Il Giappone, seconda parte dell'Asia*, cit., p. 254.

30 Hélène Vu Thanh, *Un équilibre impossible: financer la mission jésuite du Japon, entre Europe et Asie (1579–1614)*, in «Revue d'histoire moderne et contemporaine», 63/3 (2016), pp. 7–29; Ead., *Construire l'empire, développer le commerce. Le cas des missionnaires ibériques au Japon (XVI$^e$–XVII$^e$ siècles)*, in «Mélanges de la Casa de Velazquez», n.s., 50/2 (2020), pp. 241–61; Tronu Montane, *Sacred Space and Ritual in Early Modern Japan*, cit., pp. 74–78, 84–88.

31 "Es este puerto de Nagasaki muy fuerte porque tiene una punta de tierra alta que se extiende tanto por la mar que queda casi por todas partes rodeada de mar, y por la parte que se continua con la tierra está muy fortalecida con sus baluartes y cava, y en el cabo de esta punta está nuestra casa, que es como una fortaleza, apartada de lo demás del pueblo" (Valignano, *Sumario de las cosas de Japon (1583)*, cit., pp. 79–80).

32 Haruko Nawata Ward, *Women Religious Leaders in Japan's Christian Century, 1549–1650*, Farnham, Ashgate, 2009.

33 Gian Carlo Roscioni, *Il desiderio delle Indie. Storie, sogni e fughe di giovani gesuiti italiani*, Torino, Einaudi, 2001; Girolamo Imbruglia, *La milizia come «maniera di vivere» dei gesuiti: missione, martirio obbedienza*, in «Rivista di Storia del

Cristianesimo», 2 (2018), pp. 271–83; Pizzorusso, *Il martirio in odium fidei dalla realtà missionaria alla burocrazia romana*, cit., pp. 183–84.
34 Omata Rappo, *Des indes lointaines aux scènes des collèges*, cit., pp. 83–183.
35 Ivi, pp. 351–68; Sylvie Morishita, *L'art des missions catholiques au Japon (XVI$^e$–XVII$^e$ siècle)*, Paris, Les éditions du Cerf, 2020, pp. 133–39; Maria Elena Ota Mishima, *Un mural novohispano en la catedral del Cuernavaca: los veintiseis martires de Nagasaki*, in «Estudios de Asia y Africa», 16/4 (1981), pp. 675–96.
36 On the – somewhat missed – encounter between the Italian peninsula and Japanese culture, cf. Alessandro Tripepi, *Lo specchio di sé. Identità culturali e conquista spirituale nel viaggio italiano di quattro principi giapponesi alla fine del XVI secolo*, Milano, Pearson, 2022.

# 2 Planting crosses

### The conquest of sacred space

The first Jesuit missionaries landed on the southernmost island of the Japanese archipelago, Kyushu, in August 1549. It was in that area, at the time still independent from the central power, that they found the best welcome among the local feudal lords, curious about the culture and habits of those strange monks who came from the sea and would soon be nicknamed "Barbarians of the South." The daimyos of Kyushu were above all attracted to the merchandise and firearms brought by the Portuguese traders, those precious mediators with the Chinese empire.[1] And yet, those beggar clerics seemed to exercise a totally mysterious and decisive influence over the traders. For this reason, the spread of Christianity in the Land of the Rising Sun was done initially thanks to the close collaboration between Lusitanian merchants and missionaries. Moreover, it was Francis Xavier himself who understood the importance of Portuguese support in the work of persuading the Japanese princes.[2] Later, Valignano suggested to the pope to excommunicate the captains of Portuguese ships calling at the ports of lords hostile to Christianity.[3] And indeed, that solidarity between Westerners bore fruit. Within a few years, a significant number of daimyos welcomed and protected the Jesuits, allowing them to go around the lands and cities to preach the Good News. In order to ensure a sort of exclusivity in commercial relations with Western merchants, a smaller number of Japanese lords went even further, abandoning the ancient Buddhist faith and embracing the precepts of the Christian Law.

Among the first samurai princes converted were those of a reigning dynasty from Amakusa, an island opposite Arima. Having defeated his enemies, Amakusa Shigehisa (Izu-no-Kami), daimyo of Hondo, called on Father Francisco Cabral, the head of the Jesuits, to send someone to baptize him. The prince took the Christian name of Miguel – as it is mentioned in Jesuit sources – and assured his full support to the missionaries, who, according to the account of the Society's historian Daniello Bartoli, baptized "two thousand idolaters" within a few months in 1571.[4] The conversion of the prince's wife gave further impetus to the advance of Christianity. After initial hostility, struck by the "sudden change of customs" and by the "holy life of the

DOI: 10.4324/9781003275008-3

faithful," she also chose to become a Christian with the name of Gracia. In the fiefdom of Miguel and Gracia, the conversions of nobles, peasants and even Buddhist bonzes multiplied, persuaded by the sermons of Japanese Friar João, who "indoctrinated them, and there they learned to form the sign of the cross and recite their first prayers."[5] But alongside the pastoral dimension of instruction in the dictates of the new faith, the Jesuit preacher urged converts to provide tangible proof of their spiritual breakthrough – i.e., concrete actions aimed at eradicating the ancient cults considered pagan: "Nothing remained standing, neither altar, nor idol. Every memory of them wound up consumed by fire, destroyed and turned to ash. Crosses were then erected all over the place, and thirty churches were built for as many peoples."[6] Other times it happened that the crosses chose the places where to be erected: at least this is what a missionary letter dating back to 1562 tells us, when, following the appearance of a large cross in the sky, the Christians chose to plant a real one at the entrance to the port of Yokoseura, in Kyushu. Inside the inlet there was a small round island, on top of which a large cross was erected, so imposing as to be visible from a considerable distance and to guarantee an effective Christianization of the space.[7]

From the same Jesuit sources, we therefore learn that the conquest of souls was systematically followed by the conquest of sacred space,[8] through the destruction of Buddhist places of worship – temples, altars, statues – and their immediate replacement with new buildings and Christian symbols: churches and crosses.[9] On the other hand, in their worldwide expansion, Christians had everywhere marked their arrival in unknown lands by inscribing their presence with symbols such as the cross. In 1542, having arrived in Goa, on the west coast of India, Francis Xavier wrote to his companions in Rome about his journey along the African coast, where he had had the opportunity to stop in what is now Malindi, a Muslim city but full of Portuguese traders who would bury their dead in large tombs with prominent crosses. Near the city a large golden cross had then been erected, at the sight of which – alone and triumphant in the midst of so many infidels – the missionary and his traveling companions were moved.[10] Other sources confirm the importance of the cross symbol in the imagination of the missionaries, who before embarking for Japan gathered information on the cultural practices of the inhabitants of the archipelago, looking for similarities[11] and possible points of contact.[12] When the decision was actually made to embark for the Far East, the list of objects destined to accompany the first Jesuits significantly included a *"cruz de prata,"* a *"crucifixo grande de vulto,"* two other *"crucifixos meãos de vulto"* and one *"deles de pao de Sam Thomé,"* but also volumes dedicated to the cross and the passion of Christ.[13]

It is therefore not surprising that once he arrived in Japan, Francis Xavier felt the need to replicate that model of space appropriation already effected in other parts of the world by Europeans. During his passage through the Yamaguchi region, he had planted a cross, subsequently uprooted, cut and burned by the bonzes. However, the power of the cross was capable of producing phenomena of devotion even after its destruction. Bartoli tells us that an old Japanese Christian woman of over eighty, renamed Catharina, would go on feast days to wherever the future missionary saint had planted a cross to pray, and she would kiss the earth covered by the ashes of the symbol of Christ's passion. Starting from the story of an apparently marginal episode, the Jesuit historian seems to want to emphasize two elements. On the one hand, the cross somehow helps to build a sacred space all around it, the hierophany it produces in a pagan and profane landscape exerts a particular power that extends to the earth and does not disappear even with the destruction of the cross itself.[14] On the other hand, the spiritual space constituted by the cross produces a phenomenon of expansion of the sacred, which concerns human beings as well as objects. Although a laywoman, Catharina became the protagonist of a further propagation of the Christian faith, capable, through reasoning on "what she knew of the mysteries of the faith," of inducing dozens of "idolaters" to convert and be baptized.[15]

In an area of potential conversion too vast for the very few missionaries present in the Japanese archipelago, the Jesuits chose, in some cases, to delegate the work of spreading Christianity to the laity – and even to women.[16] They did so through the transmission of the sacred by means of crosses, real vectors of holiness and symbolic substitutes for priests in flesh and blood.[17] The same Jesuit sources of the time recognized the supplementary role of wooden symbols, as can be seen, for example, in a letter dated January 3, 1562, addressed by the daimyo of Kagoshima, Shimazu Takahisa. Interested in encouraging the arrival of European ships in his port, he told his missionary interlocutors about the presence of a community of converts who, to compensate for the absence of priests, had erected a large cross, even though – he specified with an evocative image – "a kingdom without priests must seem like the earth at sunset or under a cloudy sky."[18]

Analogous dynamics reappear in different contexts of Jesuit activities, as proof of a systematic and shared strategy of conquering space and souls developed by the Society of Jesus. Having obtained the permission of the temporal authorities, the priests began to preach – in early years not directly, but through Japanese converts – and to baptize hundreds of the faithful. Just as in the Europe of the Protestant Reformation and the Wars of Religion, preaching assumed a performative function; the preacher's words triggered certain attitudes on the part of the audience, prompted to transform the word into concrete actions and confirm, through iconoclastic acts, one's spiritual breakthrough.[19] Despite the will of the Jesuits, who often – at least in Bartoli's whitewashed account – tried to moderate the fervor of the new followers, inviting them to meekness and respect for their adversaries,[20] they nevertheless destroyed idols, altars and Buddhist temples,[21] persecuted the bonzes,[22] and ultimately established new symbols, with the construction of churches and chapels financed by the entire community of converts. Also, as mentioned, they erected large crosses in the fields and cities.

In Nagasaki, for example, in 1575, after having uprooted "from the foundations to the point of leaving no vestige of any temples of the idols that ever stood, from the most sumptuous to the least noble," the Christians built forty churches, and they planted "with public solemnity more than a hundred crosses, at the foot of which there was hardly ever a time that a large number of faithful were not found to revere them."[23] Crosses therefore became points of reference and meeting places for the newborn communities of Japanese Christians. But crosses were soon transformed into producers of the sacred: "God," Bartoli adds, in fact, "immediately began to respect the crosses, frequently working through them and manifesting miracles."[24] In another region of Kyushu, the kingdom of Bungo, similar episodes of miraculous conversions and healings took place, starting from the crosses planted in the fields:

> Lepers, by only kneeling at the foot of a cross planted on top of a small hill, were perfectly cleansed by the devotion of the faithful; [...] five poor blind men, in the very act of being baptized, recovered the sight of their eyes in an instant, which served to enlighten many idolaters, who were blind in soul rather than in body.[25]

Also, instead of replacing the Buddhist presence, the Christians obtained uninhabited plots of land from the local lords to be able to build their homes there. Punctually, as the first act of taking possession, the priests erected a large wooden cross, around which they organized the first community meetings for the new converts, starting from the blessing ceremony and adoration.[26]

Analogous stories can be found in the letters sent to Rome by missionaries as well as in the chronicles of the Christian conquest of the heart of the Japanese empire written by Bartoli. Indeed, during the 1570s, thanks to the initiative of Organtino Gnecchi Soldo from Brescia, the Christian faith also made its way into the streets of the imperial capital – at that time Miyako, today Kyoto – and throughout the surrounding region. The mass baptisms multiplied along with the transformation of private houses into Catholic churches thanks to the support of the new strong man of central Japan, Oda Nobunaga, the man who initiated the process of reunifying the Japanese empire, which would come to fruition a few decades later under the Tokugawa. Here, too, large crosses were promptly erected, and the religious and devotional life of the new community of the faithful would be structured around that place.[27]

The ceremony during which the crosses were planted was introduced into a community logic of reaffirming social hierarchies. For the missionaries' intents and purposes, Christianity was configured as a religion suitable for everyone, rich and poor, nobles and peasants, without distinction of social class. The new faith brought by the priests was not, in fact, reserved exclusively for poor people, who certainly appreciated its somewhat egalitarian dimension, nor only for the wealthy classes, who were able to admire its ritual and theological complexity, not to mention the undeniable economic advantages due to collaboration with Portuguese merchants and competition established with the Buddhist bonzes always thirsty for lands and riches.[28] But in his description of the ceremony, Bartoli also emphasizes another element, to which we will have the opportunity to return: namely, the link that came to be established between the cult of the cross, the re-enactment of the passion of Christ, and the development of a penitential religiosity, all much appreciated by the Japanese faithful.[29]

In addition to considerably reinvigorating the fervor of the new converts, the conquest of sacred spaces by Christian crosses implied the expulsion of the ancient gods. These gods were compared to crazed demons, who "cried through the mouths of all the possessed that this planting of Christ's crosses was an uprooting of the religion of the Kami [Shinto deities]"[30] – to the extent that the deities heralded their imminent disappearance from Japan's religious landscape and the need, which could no longer be postponed, to seek acceptance in another country. Analogous references to an entirely otherworldly struggle between the cross and the demons linked to the traditional religions of Japan, threatened by the appearance of the Christian God, can be found in a handwritten letter from Organtino, engaged, as has been said, in the propagation of the Catholic faith in the region around in Kyoto

> This year we have planted some crosses with such solemnity that it was a wonder for the gentiles, and we had determined to exult this feast of Saint Michael with the just standard of the cross to this city of Miyako along with the intercession of the glorious Virgin Mary and of Saint Michael the Archangel, to whom we especially recommend the conversion in this work; but wars and other things impede us, and with all this the battle is not lost even if it is postponed. I cannot tell Your Paternity the great hatred that the devil manifestly shows to the Most Holy Cross, speaking through his ministers who say they must destroy all the Japanese sects in which these Christians rejoice, honoring the cross in a great way with good works (which we constantly preach) to put the devil on the run.[31]

In the same months Organtino reported to Valignano the numerous conversions that had taken place in the region, which were followed by the raising of large crosses by the faithful.[32] Confident in the advance of the Christian faith, the priest from Brescia confided to his superior his ambition to take possession of one of the most important Buddhist temples, located on the heights around Kyoto and inhabited by numerous bonzes, in order to be able to "consecrate that place and make it a temple in honor of Saint Michael the Archangel," and then "to plant a very large cross in the highest one, so that it could be discovered by all Miyako and adored by everyone."[33] The importance for the missionaries of replacing the Buddhist places of worship was therefore evident, especially if their location in terms of architecture and space was dominant over the entire city. But actually, the Jesuits had to wait a few more years to fully integrate into the urban landscape of the main imperial population centers. In 1585, now permanently settled in the very heart of ancient Japan, Christians were able to manifest their presence with the raising of a large cross, an unequivocal sign of rupture with the traditional sacred landscape made up of Buddhist temples.[34] In fact, in that year the Christians built in Sakai, one of the main ports of central Japan, south of Osaka, a "very good house, perhaps the best we have here in Japan," capable of welcoming all the Christians of Miyako in case of need and revolt. "It stands in the middle of this city, on the best site with a very large and beautiful cross elevated on top of the roof," surrounded all around by four Buddhist temples. The introduction of the cross into the Japanese urban space in the mid-1580s – that is, when the persecutions had yet to begin – unequivocally attested to the influential protections enjoyed at that time by the priests of the Society, well ensconced in the courts and entourages of the powerful lords.

In addition to the places of the living, the missionaries' crosses increasingly occupied the space destined for the remains of the dead as well. In fact, since the first years of its presence in Japan, many Jesuit chronicles and letters report the systematic appearance of crosses in Christian cemeteries or their use during funeral ceremonies. For centuries a symbol of transcendence in Europe, the cross accompanied the dead on their last journey, without ceasing to speak to those who remained and would come to honor their deceased loved ones. The double function of watching over the dead and warning the living made the cross central in the funerals of Japanese converts. For example, on October 8, 1561, in Funai, where there was not yet a cemetery reserved for the followers of the new God, an impressive funeral ceremony took place in honor of an old woman who had converted. Arriving in front of her home, the priest raised a large wooden cross, which they carried in procession through the town accompanied by songs, litanies and sacred music, with the aim of paying homage to the deceased Christian and at the same time striking the imagination of the bystanders with the majesty of the ceremony.[35] Similarly, a few years earlier, in 1554, in Yamaguchi two missionaries honored a deceased Christian gentleman by crossing the entire city on foot, and then raising a large crucifix and various lights, with the aim of attracting other Japanese to the Christian faith.[36]

The funeral was a particularly propitious moment to make Christianity known to the still unconverted relatives and friends of the deceased. Thus, the valorization of the cross had the ambition, on the one hand, of speaking to the faithful, offering them a strong and easily distinguishable identity symbol; and on the other hand, it also aroused the curiosity of the pagans through the spectacle of the final farewell. Especially because the Japanese – another missionary priest tells us – unaccustomed to lavish funerals, were particularly impressed by the spectacular Jesuit scenography. Precisely for this reason, at the end of the ceremony, it was then necessary to remind them that the homage was not intended for the mortal body, but rather for the soul destined instead for eternal life.³⁷ As a moment of farewell and homage to the deceased, an opportunity to widen the audience of potential new converts, the funeral also became a means of strengthening and perfecting the faith of those who were already Christian. And the cross was always placed at the heart of this ceremony, as confirmed by the description of yet another funeral held in 1555. The Portuguese missionary Balthazar Gago took advantage of this to outline the ways in which the funerals of Christians in the Far East were usually carried out. Having received news of the death, the faithful had a wooden coffin built, paid for, in case of poverty, through a collection; then four friends of the deceased would carry the body on their shoulders, while the brother erected a crucifix and the priest intoned sacred litanies and recited Our Fathers. The procession full of lanterns formed in front of the deceased's home would accompany the corpse to the burial ground. In order to be able to conduct these ceremonies in the best possible way, the missionary expressly asked his correspondents in Europe to get him a large gold cross with a well-made crucifix that he could raise and carry in the procession.³⁸

The importance of being able to autonomously manage the transition from life to death and to strengthen their control not only over souls but also over the bodies of the deceased and related cults prompted the fathers to obtain, as soon as they arrived in a new region, a plot of land that served as a cemetery for Christians. In their correspondence, alongside the foundation of churches and hospitals – which were also transformed into places of prayer and conversion starting from the large crosses raised in front of the premises responsible for the care of the sick³⁹ – the establishment of a cemeteries appears central. For example, in the region of Hirado on September 23, 1555, the local lord granted a plot of land to the Christians so that they could gather to celebrate their festivities around a *"cruz muito grande,"* destined, however, to become a place for burial of the dead.⁴⁰

Precisely by virtue of the aggregative function they assumed for the community of converts, the crosses in the cemetery were targeted by the enemies of Christianity during the persecutions. Four years later in the same region, once the missionary fathers had been expelled, the bonzes ordered the destruction of the cross that had been raised in the cemetery. The task was carried out by three knights. It was a terrible offense for Christians – the missionary letters report – but destined not to go unpunished. The following day two of the three culprits were found dead at the foot of the broken cross, while the third knight got away.⁴¹ Even destroyed, the crosses did not lose their power and supernatural capacity for self-defense against the enemies of the faith. Just as in some cases they proved to possess surprising anti-seismic qualities, surviving devastating earthquakes that razed temples, statues and Buddhist altars to the ground.⁴²

And somehow the crosses resisted the persecutions unleashed by Hideyoshi's first anti-Christian edict, even by virtue of its only very partial application. Those large wooden symbols planted in the earth by the Jesuits remained for a long time the reference points of religious life for the communities of Japanese converts. In a letter sent to Rome at the end of 1599, the Visitor of Missions responsible for evangelization in Asia, Alessandro Valignano, reported the episode of a cross very similar to those encountered up to that point. Planted by missionaries inside a Christian cemetery, the cross soon became a destination for pilgrimages and a meeting place for the faithful, who would kneel before it to gather in prayer. At some point, visions of other shining crosses of different sizes began to appear around it, attracting a growing influx of Christians from neighboring lands:

> And for many days the flow of the people who came from various parts was so great that a multitude of noble and ignoble people went as far as the lands of Arima. And some saw several crosses, others only a single resplendent one; others saw nothing. Many arriving saw nothing but their own cross, but after having prayed a little, they saw many crosses like the others. And they appeared both during the day and at night: now on one side, now on the other, now on both sides of their own cross, which was there, and of the same size and measure; and other times they finally appeared larger.[43]

Unlike other missionaries, Valignano limited himself to recording the prodigious event but, while attributing it to a divine intervention, he did not venture explanations and preferred not to delve into the unfathomable mysteries of heaven. However, he noted with satisfaction the beneficial effects of these apparitions on the life of faith of the Christian community in the Far East: many "were moved by sorrow for their sins, weeping bitterly, confessing and making great resolutions to amend their lives"; others, on the other hand, "were greatly confirmed in the evangelical faith," thanking God for having made them worthy of such marvels. But even outside the Christian community, there were many Gentiles who were "moved to believe the Catholic truth, with the desire and fervor to become Christians growing in them."

Valignano concluded his account with the description of the intervention of the highest religious authority of the archipelago, the bishop of Nagasaki, whose attention was drawn to the constant and growing influx of faithful around that prodigious cross. Unlike other situations, which we will return to later, in this case the bishop, in concert with the missionary fathers, chose "not to want to do anything else" other than to leave free rein to the spontaneous popular devotion, since beyond the prodigious apparitions there had been no real miracles, as in cases of sudden cures. Nonetheless, the episcopal intervention ensured that the place of worship was adapted with some architectural adaptations so as to better accommodate the pilgrimages and protect the material integrity of the wooden cross. As usual, the faithful had soon detaching small pieces of it as relics to take home. The cross was therefore set in a larger one and covered by a small roof supported by four columns, so that, from the sides, Christians could continue to have access to what had now turned into a small sanctuary in the middle of a graveyard.[44] The bodies' final stop on their earthly sojourn, the grounds where the Christian community would honor their dead, was thus transformed into a privileged space of interaction between heaven and earth, where the living, gathered in prayer around the wooden cross, could experience the awesome presence of the new God.

## Symbol of a suffering God

So the cross was a sign of public distinction and affirmation of another identity, in opposition to the traditional symbols of local worship. Yet, as we have seen, the cross also became a meeting place for the community of the faithful who gathered around that symbol to pray individually or collectively, as well as on the occasion of major celebrations, like Easter, or important rites of passage, such as funerals. For example, in April 1581 the Easter procession led by Father Organtino, in crossing various cities, visited the crosses erected by the various local communities of Christians, who would gather there even more than in the church.[45] Once, in the imperial capital, in the presence of significant figures of the aristocratic elite, Organtino demanded from a Japanese nobleman guilty of having given himself up to gambling a rigorous penance complete with public flogging. On Easter Sunday, the procession, in which 15,000 Christians took part, wound its way through the streets of the center and stopped in front of a large cross, where there were "twelve armed men with very splendid white weapons, and twenty-five young men dressed as angels with paintings in their hands." However, the cross was only the central element of a more complex scenography. With great flair for theatrical entertainment, in order to impress the numerous infidels who flocked to witness the ceremony, the Jesuits resorted to sacred music – the organ was an unknown instrument in those lands – and to an impressive choreography, in which Japanese art and Christian art mixed and superimposed.[46]

> There was a beautiful coffin carried by four nobles; there were beautiful oil paintings like banners with many lanterns worked in different ways. The priest visiting from the East Indies [Valignano] carried the reliquary with the wood of the most holy cross under the canopy. The fathers with copes, chasubles, tunicles.[47]

In line with such a spectacular use of the cross symbol inserted into a complex ceremony is the report dating back to the first years of the Jesuit presence in the south of the archipelago. On October 29, 1557, Father Gaspar Vilela referred to an imposing ceremony in which he had taken part during the holy week of Easter, entirely centered on the symbolism of the cross and the exaltation of Christ's crucifixion. They preached to the faithful, including many women, about the passion and showed a crucifix to prepare them for the disciplining of the body. A procession followed, led by a large cross, accompanied by armed men and missionaries dressed in priestly robes, chanting sacred litanies. During mass, the large cross had remained outside the church, whose doors had been closed. Although they could no longer see it from inside, the faithful, accompanied by the organ, continued to answer the prayers intoned by the priest who remained with the cross, then reappeared at the end of the ceremony.[48] The Jesuits' scenic arrangement – very similar to what they did in Europe[49] – in this case provided for a studied alternation of different moments of proximity and distance, exaltation and hiding, of the Christian symbol par excellence in order to generate a feeling of communion and joy in the bystanders, interspersed with moments of anticipation.

In yet another circumstance, Father Vilela, along with Balthazar Gago, led a procession of faithful centered around a large cross. After having raised it on a hill, accompanied by armed Portuguese with torches, as well as by the music of flutes and other instruments, the two fathers went down to the port where the cross, carried in procession, resonated with other particularly bright red crosses inscribed on the banners and flags waving from the anchored ships, which fired blank artillery shots as they passed. The game of correspondences between the wooden cross and those on the flags, together with the spatial dimension of the movement of the faithful, were probably supposed to convey the sensation of a progressive conquest of space, not only sacred, by Christians. The occupation of space was pursued on the sonic level as well as the visual, through the sought-after mingling of sacred songs and musical instruments with the secular sounds of ship cannon, as if to suggest a fusion between men of God, engaged in the conquest of souls, and the men of commerce and war, ready to come to their aid in case of need. The ceremony then concluded again on the hill where the faithful had had the opportunity to listen to sermons on the value of the cross and how each could use it in their own experience of Christian life. At the end of a circular route – from the hill to the sea and back – the preached word crowned a process of proselytism and indoctrination of potential new converts, whose senses of hearing and sight had just been aroused.[50]

However, the cross was not an isolated and independent element of the Jesuit strategy for the conquest of space and souls; rather, it participated in a broadly constructed system of Christian visual symbology, together with sacred images of the Virgin and the saints. Certainly, however, from the sources, its use appears central and recurrent. Thousands of kilometers away from a Europe divided between Protestants and Catholics, the Jesuits seemed to rediscover the taste and interest in the meditation of the cross and the passion of Christ, and manifested the clear intention of converting infidels and pagans starting from the wooden object. Thus, a Christocentric spirituality took shape, reduced almost to the essentials, corresponding only in part to the Baroque complexity of the Counter-Reformation faith, of which, in Europe, the Jesuits themselves were promoters and interpreters in those years[51]. Such an attitude can be traced on the one hand to the distance from European confessional controversies and conflicts with Lutherans and Calvinists. It allowed them greater ease in resorting with more conviction to Christocentric elements of Pauline matrix,[52] which were already characteristic of the spirituality of Ignatius and the early Jesuits.[53] On the other hand, the cult of the cross and interest in the story of Christ's passion appealed in some way to the spontaneous curiosity and taste of the Japanese.

As we learn from Bartoli himself, not only did the Japanese who had already converted or those attracted by the revolutionary evangelical message flock to the sermons of the Jesuit priests, but also those who wanted to "confirm themselves in the love and esteem of their law and in the hatred and contempt of the Christian, who adores a God who is whipped and stripped naked to die on the cross."[54] The cultural distance between the followers of the Buddha and those of Christ could not have been deeper, since the torture of the cross was traditionally reserved in Japan for "ignoble and very great criminals," and, therefore, was ill-suited to a God who became man.[55] In the Land of the Rising Sun, a completely different horizon of expectation was reserved for divinities, "gods of supreme majesty and immense power, never touched by any reproachful outrage, never subjected to any suffering of death."[56] And yet, that scandalous and paradoxical story of a weak son of God, mocked, tortured and crucified by men, in some cases aroused a strong impression and exercised a form of attraction among Japanese listeners, fascinated by the eschatological dimension of universal redemption through the sufferings of a single god-man. Thus, the story of the Passion acquired a systematic centrality in the apostolate of the priests in the Far East, from which the features attributed to the symbol of the cross descended.[57]

Moreover, already at the beginning of the Jesuit adventure in Japan, Francis Xavier had noticed the specific interest aroused by the story of Christ's passion. Moved, the listeners would burst into tears and listen with extreme attention to the description of the different phases of the torture.[58] The confusion between the sacred and the profane, the divine and the human, the glorious and the miserable, seemed to destabilize the Japanese listener. In the long run, however, a theological innovation of this magnitude, so foreign to the local religious culture, ended up not taking root or even arousing a distrust that could not be recomposed; this would ultimately determine the decline of the Jesuits' dream of a Christianized Japan. Yet for several decades that bizarre mingling of such different levels, while scandalous, managed to attract and fascinate at least a part of the Japanese population. The enemies of Christianity themselves realized this, and they did not fail to underline the centrality of the use of the cross symbol in the Jesuits' religious proselytizing efforts.[59] But the episodes in which the Japanese faithful appropriated that controversial symbol, of which various Jesuit sources give an account, are also proof of this.

Planting crosses   35

The most striking testimony is certainly the development, encouraged by the fathers, of a penitential-type spirituality and devotional practice. In the pages sent from the Far East there are descriptions of processions of flagellants,[60] complete with insistence on the blood of the faithful spilled to purge one's own sins.[61] In fact, the cross and the scourge assumed absolute centrality in the construction of a Japanese Christian identity,[62] even to the detriment of alternative proposals, such as, for example, statues and images of the Virgin.[63] As demonstrated by Francis Xavier's choice to privilege the exposition of the world's creation rather than other doctrines of the Christian faith,[64] or by the typical insistence of the first Jesuit missionaries on the rational character of Christianity, presented almost as a natural rather than a revealed religion,[65] or by the place granted to the laity in the work of evangelization – unthinkable in Europe; the encounter between Japanese culture and Christian culture took place halfway, but only around certain themes and symbols, and at the price of many compromises and renunciations. And the particular attachment to a spirituality of the cross on the part of the converts emerged from various testimonies, such as, for example, the story of the escape of a Christian prince of Kyushu, who was driven out by his enemies and forced to abandon his palace and his lands. He chose to take into exile only the cross of the altar, the object most precious to him.[66] Another Christian prince, this time in the region around the ancient capital, used to carry the cross of Christ on his shoulders on Good Friday in a reenactment of the ascent to Golgotha, to the astonishment and wonder of his subjects as well as of the Jesuit priests themselves.[67]

It is not surprising that following these manifestations of attachment to the symbol of the Passion, many faithful chose to wear a cross on their chests, "some in silver, some in gold," or even "going out in public with banners in hand, in which some mystery or instrument of the Passion was portrayed either in painting or embroidery."[68] But even more astonishing was the choice of Christian warriors, daimyos and samurai, to wear the symbol of the cross on their helmets, shields and shafts, thus forming a Christian militia, we could say a sort of army of exotic crusaders with katanas in hand, ready to sacrifice their lives in the name of the faith. Arrayed in that manner, those warriors of God, who "all had a golden Jesus on their helmets and a great cross crowned with rays unfurled in their banners" before leaving for military campaigns, would gather at the church of the Jesuit priests for prayer and to obtain absolution from their sins.[69]

Before Hideyoshi's edict, the Christian daimyo Takayama Ukon, as we have seen, would also make his samurai wear the sign of the cross,[70] just as in peacetime he favored the conversion of his subjects through the distribution of cross-shaped amulets and of images of Christ to the new faithful of his lands.[71] Both in his fiefdom of Takatsuki and later in that of Akashi, the Christian daimyo favored the settlement of missionaries, the destruction of Buddhist temples, the construction of roughly a hundred churches and the raising of at least as many large crosses, as the Portuguese Jesuit Luis Piñeiro[72] and his confessor Pedro Morejón[73] recalled after the daimyo's death. Devotional ceremonies and penitential processions were organized around them, centered on the celebration of the Passion of Christ.[74] If it is true that Father Dario, as soon as he converted to Christianity, had a large wooden church built in Takatsuki with various rooms to house the missionaries, then it was a family custom. In front of the religious buildings, he had set up a garden in the center of which there was a large cross with three steps placed under the trees among various types of flowers and a fish tank, so as to constitute a suitable place of recollection and prayer for the faithful. Outside the fortress he then placed a Christian cemetery dominated by another large wooden cross.[75]

The case of Ukon therefore demonstrates the ability of the Jesuits and their great lay patrons to combine the use of the cross in a dual perspective: through it, on the one hand, they aimed at the conquest of space, both sacred and profane, in a logic of Christianizing places and buildings, and of colonizing gazes; on the other hand, small wooden crosses and other cult objects such as amulets and lucky charms allowed the faithful to appropriate the symbols of faith in a more intimate and personal way, and to nurture through them a "theology of the quotidian,"[76] centered on their needs and on the repetitive and trivial gestures of everyday life. And so it was, for example, for a Japanese from the province of Bungo, in Kyushu, who in 1555, having converted and taken the Christian name of Paulo, began to live according to the dictates of the new faith; he learned prayers and built himself a small wooden cross to always keep at hand.[77]

If the story of Ukon stands out for its importance and continuity in the panorama of the Jesuit mission in the Far East, the cases of Japanese samurai transformed into Christian crusaders can be found almost everywhere in the archipelago up until the repressive turn inaugurated in 1587 by Hideyoshi himself: knights decorated with crusader symbols,[78] warriors ready to fight under the insignia of Nobunaga, but not without having "wrapped the rosary around their helmet," "a golden Jesus on their forehead," or "the cross on their chest."[79] And again, fortresses defended not only by weapons, but by "weathervanes" with "the name of Jesus painted in the middle,"[80] as well as fleets whose sails were distinguished by the presence of banners with a "vermilion cross."[81] Several decades later, when the expulsion of the missionaries from the Japanese islands was definitive, the symbol of the cross also became, in some way, a sign of political opposition to the Tokugawa dynasty, responsible for anti-Christian persecutions, for those warriors who remained faithful to the God of the Gospel, and for this reason they took refuge under the insignia of Hideyoshi's son during the siege of Osaka in 1614–1615.[82]

There was still talk of miraculous crosses in 1616, in the wake of the nearly definitive expulsion of the missionaries from the archipelago, when the persecutions of the Tokugawa against Christians became increasingly harsh. In the image of the faithful, even the wooden symbols of their faith suffered

## Planting crosses   37

the fury of pagan persecutors:[83] the cross thus became, in the eyes of the Jesuits, the embodiment of the resistance of all Japanese Christianity against the shogun. In the months immediately following the expulsion of the last Jesuit priests, between 1615 and 1616, a cross planted "in times of past persecutions had remained standing" and was held in great veneration by the faithful for its thaumaturgical qualities – "those struck by malarial fever chopped a few pieces into crumbs, and by drinking it infused in water, they often recovered their health." For fear that "like other crosses it would be destroyed" by order of the shogun, it was hidden underground by a "good Christian."[84] Despite the precaution, it was finally discovered and set on fire by the persecutors. A few days later the same faithful who had tried to save the object of worship, looking out the window of the house at the place where the cross had stood for a long time, could see "above that spot an unusual light measuring a good ten feet square"; that "splendor was so great that it radiated around the sight for some twenty paces, so that everything was distinctly seen there, and that splendor lasted as long as five Our Fathers and Hail Marys." The believer was thus convinced that it was a positive omen announcing the imminent rise of a new cross.

This last example shows us the survival of the symbol of the cross even in the age of persecution. It also reveals that the strategy of conquering space pursued through the symbol was not only linked to a transposition on the other side of the globe of a Counter-Reformation sensibility, aggressive and intolerant of other people's religions; it was also the expression of a transformation and an adaptation, at least in part surprising, of Jesuit spirituality in a new and distant context. In old Europe, riven by the confessional split with the Protestants, the Jesuits in fact preferred to resort with caution to Christocentric models of piety, similar to the rival confession, and chose to insist on the centrality of the cult of the Virgin and the saints. If anything, the faithful who remained in the fold of the Roman Church could legitimately expect, as indeed happened in the Bolognese countryside, pontifical edicts hostile to the large crosses that for centuries farmers had erected in the fields as sort of talismans to protect the crops.[85] These crosses were part of daily life as well as the mental and physical landscape of the Italian countryside, crosses that nourished a faith as ancient as it was superstitious, at least in the eyes of the Church, with roots in pre-Christian cults typical of agro-pastoral societies,[86] on which the stern and disciplinary gaze of the Catholic reformers would not be slow to rest. Used as scarecrows, at the feet of which farmyard animals used to deposit their excrement, those crosses, however, had certainly lost part of their sacred power in the eyes of the old Christians of the Po valley.

Yet in the same years that the Jesuits were planting crosses in the cities and countryside of Japan, in Europe torn apart by the wars of religion, similar ceremonies of reappropriation of the space occupied by the enemies of the faith became characteristics of another religious order born precisely from the crisis of sixteenth-century Catholicism, almost in parallel with the Society of Jesus. In the southeast of France from the mid-1570s, at the invitation of the regent Catherine de' Medici, the first Capuchins arrived with the intention of reconquering the souls of those lands in which the Huguenot heresy had taken deep roots. After sending a preacher to captivate the crowds, the Capuchins would erect a large wooden cross in front of the place chosen as a future convent, often in front of the cathedral or some other important church in the city. The raising of the cross thus became a symbolic moment for the new order to enter the community, where it engaged in works of charity, assisted the poor and sick, and distinguished itself by its ascetic lifestyle inspired by the example of Saint Francis. For the Jesuits in Japan – as well as in Toulouse, Béziers, Agde and the other cities of southern France – the ceremony was attended by the highest ecclesiastical and political authorities, as well as exponents of other religious orders, and provided for a majestic staging with musical accompaniment of drums and flutes, sacred hymns and sometimes even cannon and musket shots.[87] In the history of the Capuchins themselves, those crosses became sentinels of the Catholic fortress in lands dominated by Protestants, capable of miraculously repulsing enemy soldiers and making them retreat, as happened in Montpellier in 1609.[88] Another public ritual staged by the Capuchins revolved around the cross: one of them would cross the streets of the city where they had chosen to settle, carrying a large wooden cross in one hand and a torch in the other, preceded by a brother who warned the faithful of his arrival with a bell.[89]

The choice of the cross depended on two reasons. The first, controversially, was linked to the need to respond to the destruction and looting of churches and monasteries by the Huguenots, who in their purifying fury would ravish relics, statues and depictions of the Virgin and saints, but who sometimes did spared not even the crucifixes – in their eyes also expressions of papal superstition.[90] This happened, for example, in Paris in 1547, in Puy two years later, where the crucifix was repeatedly damaged, and again in Bordeaux in 1559.[91] Planting a cross in the public space violated by heretics was therefore a militant and reparatory gesture, a way of reaffirming the presence of true faith and the legitimacy of the cult of images, of re-establishing the *ordo rerum*, of challenging opponents proposing an alternative identity and of breaking with theirs, but also of starting a new era in which the protagonists became members of a renewed Catholicism, free from the errors and abuses of the pre-conciliar clergy.[92] During the wars of religion, and also in the first decades of the seventeenth century, Capuchin friars could be seen at the head of royal armies, hurling themselves with crucifix in hand against Huguenot fortresses, as proof of the identification between the symbol of the cross and a Counter-Reformation Catholicism devoted to a fight without quarter against the heretics.[93] However, the choice of the cross rather than statues of the Virgin or of particular saints also depended on a less obvious reason, which had to do with the history of the origins of Capuchin spirituality. It arose during the 1520s out of a controversy within the Franciscan order; the new order made asceticism, humility and the model of Christ's passion – the almighty God incarnated himself as a suffering man to atone for the sins of men – the horizon of its activity and spirituality. In those years, Christocentric positions and adherence to the doctrine of justification by faith alone, which made the sacrifice of Christ the pivot of salvation, were widespread in a part of the Catholic revival, especially among the ranks of evangelical and spiritual movements. The first Capuchins were also linked to this sensitivity, especially in the years when Bernardino Ochino was vicar-general. Ochino was an extraordinary preacher and leading figure of the Catholic revival before moving on to the Reformation after his summons to Rome by the Roman Inquisition in 1542.[94]

In sixteenth-century Japan, in the presence of an analogous competition for space with other religious doctrines, the attitude of the Jesuits was no different: on the one hand, planting a cross was the expression of a Catholic identity and conquest, eager to distinguish itself and to break with the ritual and iconographic forms of the ancient religions of the archipelago; but on the other hand, the semantic and spiritual reinvestment in the symbol of Christ's passion by the Jesuits in the Far East meant something else as well. The decision to attribute absolute centrality to the cross in the process of Christianization of the Japanese countryside and cities was not only the result of an imposition; it was the result of a sort of compromise, of negotiation and mutual contamination between the variegated and flexible theological and symbolic baggage available to the priests (the cult of the cross was preferred to that of the saints and the Virgin, for example) and the sacred imagination of the converted populations. These people had been accustomed for centuries to the competitive coexistence of different faiths, and they knew how to appropriate the pervasive Christian message through the symbols par excellence of human and divine suffering.[95] In some way, the accommodating Jesuits' intuition to focus on certain symbolic motifs which referred, beyond the complex conceptual and theological elaborations they had undergone, to analogous modalities of experience and the relationship with superhuman reality was successful.[96] They were thus capable of overcoming religious and cultural barriers and putting apparently irreconcilable worlds into communication.[97]

However, the evolution of the Japanese political context, with the rise of Hideyoshi and the beginning of the persecutions, compromised the fortunes of missionary Christianity and forced the missionary fathers to a radical change of perspective. Threatened with expulsion, they had to develop more cautious and much less extravagant evangelizing strategies. The time of the great crosses erected on the hills, in the fields and in the cities of the Land of the Rising Sun as an act of defiance to the ancient gods was coming to an ineluctable end.

## Notes

1 Ninomiya, *Le Japon pré-moderne, 1573–1867*, cit., pp. 39–41.
2 *La découverte du Japon, 1543–1552. Premiers témoignages et premières cartes*, cit., pp. 263–64; on the connection between economic interests and the diffusion of the new faith cf. Adriana Boscaro, *Ventura e sventura dei gesuiti in Giappone (1549–1639)*, Venezia, Libreria Editrice Cafoscarina, 2008, pp. 37–38.
3 Ivi, pp. 38–39.
4 Jaime González-Bolado, *La intromisión de los jesuitas en la política japonesa: el caso de la rebelión de Amakusa (1589–1590)*, in «Estudios de Asia y África», 58/1 (2023), pp. 35–64; Vu Thanh, *Devenir Japonais*, cit., pp. 67–68; Steichen, *Les daimyō chrétiens*, cit., pp. 49–51. See also Luís Fróis, *Historia de Japam*, ed. José Wicki, Lisboa, Nuno Camarinhas et Tiago C.P. dos Reis Miranda, 1976, II, pp. 228–32.
5 Bartoli, *Dell'Historia della Compagnia di Giesù. Il Giappone, seconda parte dell'Asia*, cit., p. 17.
6 Ivi.
7 *Monumenta Historica Japoniae III. Documentos del Japón, 1558–1562*, ed. Juan Ruiz de Medina S.J., Roma, Instituto Historico de la Compañía de Jesús, 1995, p. 572; Castel-Branco, Carvalho, *Luis Fróis: First Western Accounts of Japan's Gardens, Cities and Landscapes*, cit., pp. 189–90.
8 For a reflection on the controversial concept of sacred space cf. Natale Spineto, *"Spazi sacri" e storia delle religioni*, in «Historia religionum», 8 (2016), pp. 15–24.
9 On the example of Nagasaki cf. Tronu Montane, *Sacred Space and Ritual in Early Modern Japan*, cit., pp. 15–18, 21–47.
10 "De Maçanbique a Goa pusimos más de dos messes. Pasamos por una ciudad de moros, los quales son de pazes: llámase la ciudad Milinde, en la qual el más de tienpo suele aver mercaderes portugeses; y los cristianos, que ay mueren, entiérranse en unas tunbas grandes, las quales hazen con cruzes. Junto con esta ciudad hizieron los portugeses una cruz grande de piedra, dorada, muy hermosa. En verla, Dios nuestro Señor sabe quánta consolación recebimos, conociendo quán grande es la virtud de la cruz, viéndola así sola y con tanta vitoria entre tanta morería" (20 September 1542; Francisco Xavier, *Epistolae S. Francisci Xaverii aliaque eius scripta*, ed. Georg Schurhammer, Josef Wicki, Romae, apud Monumenta Historica Soc. Iesu, 1945–1996, 2 vol., vol. 1: 1535–1548, p. 122).
11 The case narrated by Giovanni Botero of a Christianisation of a cross already venerated in Mexico is noteworthy: "Nell'isola di Acuzamila, che è vicina al Iucatan [Yucatan], si vede in un luogo eminente, una croce alta più di due braccia, che i paesani con gran riverenza veneravano come cosa celeste, e vi facevano ricorso, ogni volta, che in grandi siccità havevano bisogno di pioggia, né si poté mai sapere l'origine, o l'autore di così fatta religione. Si scrive anche che si sono trovate delle croci nel Iucatan, e in altre Provintie, ma per mancamento d'autorità sofficiente, io non l'oso affermare" (Giovanni Botero, *Discorso de vestigii et argomenti della fede catholica, ritrovati nell'India da' Portoghesi, e nel mondo nuovo da' Castigliani*, Roma, Appresso Giovanni Martinelli, 1588, p. 19).
12 "Adomandato se tengono alcun segno per sua difesa contra li dimonii, disse che acostumano fare nove signali in anze de si con la mano dextra de la manera che noi pintamo la croce de Santo Andrea, e facendo quelli segni dicono nove parole diverse, le quale non le intendeno se non li literati" (Informative letter on Japan by Niccolò Lancillotto, Kochi, 28 December 1548, in *Monumenta Historica Japoniae II. Documentos del Japón, 1547–1557*, ed. Juan Ruiz de Medina S.J., Roma, Instituto Historico de la Compañía de Jesús, 1990, p. 58).

13 Ivi, pp. 480, 485, 486.
14 For analogous cases of persistence of the sacred in the ashes cf. Mircea Eliade, *Traité d'histoire des religions*, Paris, Payot, 1949, pp. 268–69.
15 Bartoli, *Dell'Historia della Compagnia*, cit., p. 24.
16 Vu Thanh, *Devenir Japonais*, cit., pp. 156–74; Ward, *Women Religious Leaders in Japan's Christian Century, 1549–1650*, cit.
17 Bartoli, *Dell'Historia della Compagnia*, cit., p. 24.
18 "A este reino, ainda que pequeno, devem os padres nabangisc de folgar de vir a ele. Porque se pola ventura em outras partes acharem marée vasia, este reino a tem sempre chea. E enquanto os christãos não vem padres que aqui estejão com eles, tanto se consolão com a cruz que têm alevantada como se quá os tiveram. E imagino eu que estar ho meu reino sem padres, que hé estar o ceo toldado, ou o sol posto em eclipse e sem ninhuma claridade" (*Monumenta Historica Japoniae III*, cit., p. 486).
19 The destruction of the temples was considered by the converts a test of faith and real conversion (Bartoli, *Dell'Historia della Compagnia*, cit., p. 74).
20 Ivi, p. 32.
21 Fróis, *Historia de Japam*, cit., I, pp. 282–83; Kouamé, *Le christianisme à l'épreuve du Japon médiéval*, cit., pp. 145–75.
22 Bartoli, *Dell'Historia della Compagnia*, cit., pp. 34, 44–45.
23 Ivi, pp. 34–36.
24 Ivi, p. 35.
25 "Lebbrosi, con solo inginocchiarsi a pie' d'una croce piantata in cima d'un collicello per divozion de' fedeli, perfettamenti mondati; [...] cinque poveri ciechi, nell'atto medesimo del battezzarsi, in istanti ricoverarono la veduta de gli occhi: che valse ad illuminare molti idolatri, ch'erano ciechi dell'anima più che quegli del corpo" (ivi, pp. 79–80); on a miraculous cross that heals lepers cf. also *Alcune lettere delle cose del Giappone dell'anno 1579 infino al 1581*, Roma, Francesco Zannetti, 1584, pp. 84–85.
26 *Monumenta Historica Japoniae II*, cit., pp. 418–19, 423.
27 "Le croci poi si piantarono in ciascun luogo la sua, e in solo Cunocuni più di cinquanta. Queste, lavorate da' più eccellenti maestri che, come abbiam detto, nel Giappone, con lo scarpello in legno, fanno opere di maraviglia, nondimeno aveano il lor più bello nella pietà de' fedeli, massimamente in quell'atto publico e solenne di portarle al luogo prefisso e piantarvele. Era privilegio solo del principe, se ve ne avea, e de' figliuoli e congiunti per sangue o de' più degni per nobiltà e per grado recarsele su le spalle, con dietro il popolo, secondo diversi affetti, diversamente in abito" (Bartoli, *Dell'Historia della Compagnia*, cit., p. 129).
28 In this sense it is not surprising that especially in the first years of Christian presence in Japan the crosses found acceptance, at first, in the private homes of wealthy converted lords; for example, in the region of Hakata in 1562 the first large cross was erected in the patio of a gentleman, who then let the Christians of the region gather in prayer around it (*Monumenta Historica Japoniae III*, cit., p. 560).
29 Bartoli, *Dell'Historia della Compagnia*, cit., p. 129.
30 Ivi.
31 "Quest'anno abbiamo piantati alcuni croci con tanta solennità che fu cosa di meraviglia per gli gentili et avevamo determinato di dare uno grandissimo assalto questa festa di Santo Miguel con o dito standoro della cruce a questa città dello Miaco con la intercessione della gloriosa Virgine Maria et di Santo Michel Arcangelo alli quali andiamo raccomandati in questa opera specialmente della conversione, ma le guerre et altre cose ci impidirno con tutto questo non si perdé la battaglia anchorché si differisca. Non posso dire a Vostra Paternità il grande odio che il demonio manifestamente mostra alla Santissima cruce parlando negli suoi

ministri et dicendo che ha da destruire tutte le sette degli giaponi con che si rallegrano in grande maniera questi cristiani et se animano a honorarla con le buone opere (cosa che gli predicamo di continuo) per mettere in maggior fuga il diavolo." (Organtino to Father Everard Mercurian Superior General of the Society of Jesus, Miyako, 29 September 1577, in Archivum Romanum Societatis Iesu, *Jap.Sin.*, 8, I, ff. 177*r*–78*v*).

32 *Lettere dell'India orientale, scritte da' reverendi padri della Compagnia di Giesù*, Venezia, Antonio Ferrari, 1580, p. 323.
33 Ivi, pp. 323–24.
34 ARSI, *Jap.Sin*, 10, I, f. 91*r*, Organtino to Claudio Acquaviva, Sakai 6 December 1585. On Sakai cf. Castel-Branco, Carvalho 2020, pp. 177–82.
35 "Y en lhegando allá siempre nos vestimos quatro ou 5 de sobrepelizes, o portugueses o japanes. Donde antes que saquen al defunto de su casa ay las más veses predicatión, assí a los christianos como a gentiles que están presentes, sobre un punto de la muerte corporal y spiritual. Y después, echas las sirimonias que se acostumbran em tal caso hazer, salimos com la crus levantada delante y el defunto atrás, y nós en medio diziendo una ladainha – a la qual responden quasi todos los christianos – asta la queva, que está fuera de la ciudad em lugares detriminados antiguamente, donde se entierran. Porque aquí em Bungo aún no tenemos semiterio detriminado para los christianos como lo tienen los de Firando y Yamaguchi" (*Monumenta Historica Japoniae III*, cit., p. 431).
36 "Os de casa todos estam de saude. Véspora de Santos Cosmo e Damiam faleceu Ambrosio, cunhado de Faxissumes, que foi veador dei-rei. Forom comingou a o enterrar mais de 200 christãos, entre homens e molheres. Fui com a sobrepelicel e estola, e Melchior com sobrepelice e hum crucifixo. E andamos toda a cidade de Yamanguchi por estar a casa longe; à tornada, com a tumba alta e luminárias que era mais claro que ho dia. E asi o enterremos com a mais solenidade que pude. Donde seus parentes e a maior parte de Yamanguchi estam alvoroçados pera se fazerem christãos se ouver quem lhes pregue" (*Monumenta Historica Japoniae II*, cit., p. 460).
37 *Monumenta Historica Japoniae II*, cit., p. 699.
38 "Pera isto desejo huma cruz dourada, com hum crucifixo mui bem feito, com seu pé, que se possa alevantar em huma procisão destas quando imos a enterrar" (*Monumenta Historica Japoniae II*, cit., p. 559).
39 "E vindo a noite foi a presição com muitas candeias à santa Mizericórdia, que está em hum campo onde está aguora huma fremosa cruz alevantada e cerquada com degraos de pedras; e ali se detiverão hum pedaço em oração. Na igreja ficarão japõis armados que guardavão o moimento" (Luis de Almeida to Antonio de Quadros, Funai 1 October 1561, in *Monumenta Historica Japoniae III*, cit., pp. 377–78).
40 *Monumenta Historica Japoniae II*, cit., pp. 550, 569.
41 *Monumenta Historica Japoniae III*, cit., pp. 147, 161, 202, 285, 290.
42 "I tempii dei Fotochi et heremiti, che stavano in un luogo alto, lontano dall'istessa villa, tutti andarno a terra, e i Fotochi si fecero in pezzi [...] Nel regno di Ecunoquni era una Chiesa con una Croce sull'Altare, laquale perciò si chiamava la Chiesa di Santa Croce, e se ben cadette la Chiesa, nondimeno la Croce rimase in piedi sopra l'Altare, come stava prima" (Luis Fróis, *Trattato d'alcuni prodigii occorsi l'anno M.D.XCVI nel Giappone*, In Milano, Nella stamparia del q. Pacifico Pontio, 1599, p. 43).
43 "E tanto grande fu per molti giorni il concorso del popolo che da varie parti veniva, ch'insino alle terre d'Arima, vi andò gran numero di gente nobile et ignobile. Et alcuni vedevano diverse croci, altri una sola risplendente; altri non vedevano niente. Molti arrivando non vedevano altro che la propria croce, ma dopo d'haver fatto un

Planting crosses 43

poco d'oratione, vedevano molte croci come gli altri. Et apparivano tanto di giorno quanto di notte: et hora da una, hora dall'altra, et hora dall'una e dall'altra banda della propria croce, ch'ivi era, e della medesima grandezza e misura: et altre volte finalmente apparivano maggiori" (Valignano to Acquaviva, 10 October 1599, in *Lettera del padre Alessandro Valignano, visitatore della Compagnia di Giesù nel Giappone e nella Cina de' 10 d'ottobre del 1599, al reverendo padre Claudio Aquaviva, Generale della medesima Compagnia*, in Milano, Per l'herede del quond. Pacifico Pontio, et Gio Battista Piccaglia compagni, 1603, p. 38).
44 Ivi, p. 39.
45 *Alcune lettere delle cose del Giappone. Dell'anno 1579 insino al 1581*, Roma, Francesco Zannetti, 1584, pp. 137–38.
46 On the role of processions in the expansion of the sacred and the overlap with ancient Japanese festivals cf. Tronu Montane, *Sacred Space and Ritual in Early Modern Japan*, cit., pp. 62–67.
47 "Vi era una bara bellissima portata da quattro nobili; vi erano quadri bellissimi ad oglio a modo di stendardi con moltissime lanterne lavorate in diversi modi. Il padre visitatore delle Indie orientali [Valignano] portava il reliquario col legno della santissima croce sotto al baldacchino. I padri con piviali, pianete, tonicelle" (ivi, p. 139).
48 "Chegado a Somana Sancta, scilicet, dia [de] Ramos, fizemos com muita gente de que ha igreja estava chea, com muita solemnidade. Primeirameate benzerão-se os ramos com ha missa cantada, e depois de repartidos saimos em proção por hum terreiro que tinhamos diante da porta, com cruz alevantada, com grandissema alegria. A volta fiquou o padre com a cruz de fora e dixemos os versos cantados conforme ao que se faz na sancta madre Igreja, com as portas fechadas. E dizendo o padre *Attolite* lhe respondião de dentro em canto d'orgão com muita devação. E acabadas as três vezes se abrió a porta, de que resultou em todos grande alegria. Indo em procissão ao altar se começou a missa, e vindo ao tempo da Paixão começou a vozes de canto d'orgão" (*Monumenta Historica Japoniae II*, cit., p. 693).
49 In another letter, describing a similar procession with tambourines and flutes, the missionary wrote in fact: "Se fez hua procissão dia da Cruz *que parecia que estávamos em Portugal*, com irem todos os christãos com suas velas de cera nas maos, com averem frautas e charamelas e muitas bombardadas e espingardadas" (*Monumenta Historica Japoniae III*, cit., p. 291).
50 *Monumenta Historica Japoniae II*, cit., pp. 711–12.
51 Ucerler, *The Samurai and the Cross*, cit., pp. 47–50.
52 It should be emphasized that the systematic recourse to the raising of large crosses was not exclusive to the Jesuit mission in Japan, but is also found elsewhere, for example in India (*Lettere dell'India orientale, scritte da' reverendi padri della Compagnia di Giesù*, 1580, pp. 91–92, 115, 154). For example, Botero writes: "In tutte le parti del mondo nuovo si adoravano idoli [...] Rispondevano questi idoli alle domande di cose occolte, e di avvenimenti futuri, ma da che i christiani arrivarono là, e vi predicarono l'evangelio, e'l nome di Giesù Christo, i demonii spaventati dalle croci che vi furono piantate, e dalla presenza di Dio nell'Eucarestia, non danno più risposta" (Botero, *Discorso de vestigii et argomenti della fede catholica*, cit., p. 21).
53 Mongini, *Maschere dell'identità*, cit., pp. 313–71.
54 "confermarsi nell'amore e stima della lor legge e nell'odio e dispregio della cristiana, la quale adora un Dio frustato, messo ignudo a morire in croce" (Bartoli, *Dell'Historia della Compagnia*, cit., p. 132).
55 For this reason, according to Bourdon, the Jesuits in Japan used the cross more than the crucifix, to avoid the assimilation between the suffering Christ and the

common criminals (Léon Bourdon, *La compagnie de Jésus et le Japon. La fondation de la mission japonaise par François-Xavier (1547–1551) et les premiers résultats de la prédication chrétienne sous le supériorat de Cosme de Torres (1551–1570)*, Lisboa, Fondation Calouste Gulbenkian, Centre culturel portugais – Paris, Commission nationale pour les commémorations des découvertes portugaises, 1993 p. 615).

56 "iddi di somma maestà e d'immenso potere, non tocchi mai da niun oltraggio di vitupero, non suggetti a niun patimento di morte" (Bartoli, *Dell'Historia della Compagnia*, cit., p. 132).

57 Precisely for this reason, Bartoli argues: "Sì maestoso e solenne era quel piantare che i fedeli facevano delle croci, come innanzi dicemmo, perché oltre a sodisfare in ciò alla lor propria divozione, i gentili, in sol vederli, più che a qualunque gran predica, erano illuminati dal cielo e si facevano a conoscere che d'altro pregio, ch'essi non imaginavano, dovea essere il nostro Iddio, di cui quel medesimo che parea dispregevole, e vergognoso, com'è lo strumento del supplicio di che morì, tanto degnamente, si onorava" (ibid.).

58 *Nuovi avisi delle Indie di Portugallo ricevuti questo anno del 1553, dove si tratta della conversione di molte persone principali...*, Roma, Valerio Dorico e Luigi Fratelli, [1553], pp. Bv rv, Cvi r; Kouamé, *Le christianisme à l'épreuve du Japon médiéval*, cit., pp. 64–65.

59 Ivi, pp. 103–9.

60 *Monumenta Historica Japoniae II*, cit., p. 725.

61 As soon as he landed, Francis Xavier left the first converts in Kagoshima "*mais humas disciplinas suas*" to flog the body (Fróis, *Historia de Japam*, cit., I, p. 25).

62 On the centrality of the cross and crucifixion cf. also Omata Rappo, *Des indes lointaines aux scènes des collèges*, cit., pp. 248–89.

63 From the earliest years, the Jesuits attempted to introduce the cult of the Virgin, leaving the faithful an "*imagem pequena de N. Senhora*" (Fróis, *Historia de Japam*, cit., I, p. 25).

64 Francis Xavier to fellow residents in Europe, Cochin, January 29, 1552 in Francis Xavier, *Epistolae S. Francisci Xaverii aliaque eius scripta*, ed. Georg Schurhammer, Josef Wicki, Romae, apud Monumenta historica Soc. Iesu, 1996, vol. 2: 1549–1552, pp. 264–65.

65 Ivi, pp. 265–67.

66 *Alcune lettere delle cose del Giappone. Dell'anno 1579 insino al 1581*, cit., p. 42; Bartoli, *Dell'Historia della Compagnia*, cit., p. 76. Almost identical is the story relating to another fleeing convert, a certain Tommaso, dating back to 1557 (*Monumenta Historica Japoniae II*, cit., p. 720).

67 Bartoli, *Dell'Historia della Compagnia*, cit., p. 133.

68 *Ibidem*.

69 *Ibidem*.

70 See *supra*, cap. 1.

71 Morishita, *L'art des missions catholiques au Japon (XVIe-XVIIe siècle)*, cit., pp. 215–16.

72 "Edificaron muchas iglesias en todas sus tierras, levantaron muchas cruzes por los montes y caminos, fueron sempre exemplo a los christianos" (Luis Piñeiro, *Relacíon del suceso que tuvo nuestra santa fe en los Reinos del Japón, desde el año de seiscientos y doce hasta el de seicscientos y quince*, Madrid, 1617, p. 358).

73 "Y es cossa savida y çierta que en el dicho su estado tenia çerca de çient yglesias y capillas, y otras tantas cruzes levantadas en lugares públicos" (in *Summarium*

*documentorum*, in *Positio della causa di beatificazione di Justus Takayama Ukon*, p. 560). Allow me here to sincerely thank the postulator Father Anton Witwer, for having generously offered me the opportunity to consult the documentation of the process not yet accessible to scholars.
74 *Ibidem*.
75 Castel-Branco, Carvalho, *Luis Fróis: First Western Accounts of Japan's Gardens, Cities and Landscapes*, cit., pp. 170–71.
76 The competing contexts of bi-confessional landscapes, such as sixteenth-century Europe following the Lutheran revolt, lend themselves to creative and original forms of experimentation and construction of hybrid identities on the level of religious and cultural practices, starting from daily needs of the faithful. Cf. Silvana Seidel Menchi, *Erasmo in Italia, 1520–1580*, Torino, Bollati Boringhieri, 2001 [1987], pp. 92–94; Olivier Christin, Yves Krumenacker (ed.), *Les protestants à l'époque moderne. Une approche anthropologique*, Rennes, Presses Universitaires de Rennes, 2017.
77 *Monumenta Historica Japoniae II*, cit., p. 519.
78 Bartoli, *Dell'Historia della Compagnia*, cit., p. 100.
79 Ivi, p. 151.
80 Ivi, p. 28.
81 Ivi, p. 72.
82 "Si videro in campo di Fideyori sei bandiere con la Croce, e con l'imagini del Salvatore e di S. Iacopo; le quali insegne quanto buon sangue dovessero fare a Daifù, si può ciascuno imaginare vedendole egli inalberate, e spiegate per trargli il buono et il cattivo sangue che havea contro esse" (*Lettere annue del Giappone, China, Goa et Ethiopia, scritte a M.R.P. generale della Compagnia di Giesù, da padri dell'istessa Compagnia negli anni 1615. 1616. 1617. 1618. 1619*, in Napoli, Per Lazaro Scoriggio, 1621, p. 26).
83 For example in 1604 Tokugawa ordered that "cruces in multis locis publicae venerationis causa erectas detrahi, Christianos a fide retrocedere [...] Quo factum est, ut pus quam viginti ecclesiae veldestructae vel saltem Christianis subtractae, et multae cruces dirutae sint" (in *Monumenta Historica Japoniae I. Textus catalogorum Japoniae aliaeque de personis dunibusque S.J. in Japonia informationes et relationes 1549–1654*, ed. Josef Franz Schütte S.J., Romae, Apud Monumenta Historica Soc. Iesu, 1975, p. 499).
84 *Lettere annue del Giappone, China, Goa et Ethiopia*, cit., p. 57.
85 Adriano Prosperi, *Croci nei campi, anime alla porta. Religione popolare e disciplina tridentina nelle campagne padane del Cinquecento*, in Id., *Eresie e devozioni. La religione italiana in età moderna*, vol. *3, Devozioni e conversioni*, Roma, Edizioni di Storia e Letteratura, 2010, pp. 334–53.
86 Eliade, *Traité d'histoire des religions*, cit., pp. 211–31.
87 Barbara B. Diefendorf, *Planting the Cross. Catholic Reform and Renewal in Sixteenth and Seventeenth Century France*, New York, Oxford University Press, 2019, pp. 66–72.
88 Ivi, pp. 79–80.
89 Ivi, p. 73.
90 Ivi, pp. 78–79, 153.
91 Olivier Christin, *Une révolution symbolique. L'iconoclasme huguenot et la reconstruction catholique*, Paris, Les éditions de Minuit, 1991, pp. 186–88, 193.
92 Ivi, p. 190; Diefendorf, *Planting the Cross*, cit., p. 86.
93 Ivi, pp. 83–84.

94 Guillaume Alonge, Massimo Firpo, *Il Beneficio di Cristo e l'eresia italiana del '500*, Roma-Bari, Laterza, 2022; Michele Camaioni, *Il vangelo e l'Anticristo. Bernardino Ochino tra francescanesimo ed eresia (1487–1547)*, Bologna, Il Mulino-Istituto italiano per gli studi storici, 2018.
95 On conversion as the fruit of negotiation cf. the preface by Claude Prudhomme to Kouamé, *Le christianisme à l'épreuve du Japon médiéval*, cit., pp. vi–xii.
96 On the universality of the symbol of the cross cf. Julien Ries, *Cross*, in Mircea Eliade (ed.), *The Encyclopedia of Religion*, New York, MacMillan Publishing Company, 1987, IV, pp. 155–66; Id., *Simbolo. Le costanti del sacro*, in Id., *Opera Omnia*, Milano, Jaca Book, 2008, vol. IV/1, pp. 188–94.
97 On the existence of "structural invariants" of the religious phenomenon, see Giovanni Filoramo, *Che cos'è la religione. Temi, metodi, problemi*, Torino, Einaudi, 2004, pp. 218–19.

# 3 The miraculous tree

A beautiful seventeenth-century Japanese screen, now kept in the Itsuo museum in Ikeda, not far from Osaka, depicts the church of the Our Lady of the Assumption in Nagasaki – perched on a promontory at the entrance to the bay and clearly visible from approaching ships.[1] However, another detail of the reproduced image attracts our attention, namely the presence of some majestic trees next to the church. The description of the entrance to Nagasaki corresponds precisely to what was reported by a Dutch explorer who was in the service of the archbishop of Goa for some years and who appears very well documented on the commercial routes of the Portuguese in Asia and the Far East. To those who were destined to lead their boat into the port of Nagasaki to drop anchor, the author advised to keep the Jesuit church and, precisely, the large tree next to it as waymarks. Considered by the Japanese themselves an architectural work of considerable value, and one of the buildings to visit for a foreigner, the church had been built for the first time in 1571, on the occasion of the settlement of the priests in the region, and subsequently rebuilt several times according to the local style, in such a way as to camouflage it so as to blend in with the houses and other city buildings, despite keeping the large cross at the top as a distinctive sign.[2] In the last decades of the sixteenth century, the beginning of the persecutions had in fact pushed the Jesuits not to flaunt their presence on Japanese soil too much, and to move with discretion, even in terms of occupying space. But in addition to a modification of the structure of its buildings, the process of accommodating local tastes, styles and customs also involved a reinvestment of some traditional symbols of Japanese culture, including the tree.[3]

For people of the past, whether it was ancient Mesopotamia, Europe in the first centuries of Christianity or medieval Japan, nature was always supernatural as well, full of religious meanings. This is because throughout history the supernatural has been grasped by religious man through the natural aspects of the cosmos. In it, not all elements are equal, and the undoubted centrality of the sky, the sun, the earth and water is accompanied, in almost every culture, by that of the tree. Often the cosmos itself is represented through the image of a gigantic tree that suggests the totality of cosmic life, and at the same

DOI: 10.4324/9781003275008-4

time restores the idea of the rhythm of the seasons and of the vegetation that periodically dies and is reborn. Through the tree one enters the mystery of eternal youth, otherworldly salvation, resurrection and immortality. With its roots firmly planted on the ground and its branches reaching toward the sky, the tree assumes the value of an access key to the mystery of life which is continually renewed. At the same time, it is an element which connects various levels of the universe, acting as a stairway, an entry into the supernatural. It is no coincidence that the tree acquires a central role in many religions and cultures: in Germanic mythology the cosmic tree appears, in Mesopotamia the tree of life, in Asia the tree of immortality or Wisdom, in Iran and India the tree of youth.[4]

In Christian religious culture, the symbolism of the tree does not disappear, but is somehow recovered and integrated into a new narrative. In the Bible, in line with the Mesopotamian civilizations, the tree occupies a central space. For the first man and woman in Eden, the trees' fruits were the main, if not exclusive, source of nourishment, and the center of the garden was dominated by the Tree of Life (Gen. 2.9-16). Another tree, however, of the knowledge of good and evil – "good to eat and pleasing to the eye and... enticing for the wisdom that it could give" (Gen. 3.6) – later also became the "tree of death," according to the formula used in some rabbinical commentaries,[5] as the origin of their sin and misfortune. Adam and Eve hid "among the trees of the garden," seeking refuge from their father's interrogations (Gen. 3.8).[6] The Judeo-Christian world, therefore, establishes a complex, somewhat ambiguous relationship with the tree, which is the origin of Adam's temptation but also the prefiguration of Christ's cross,[7] and in this sense the key to man's liberation and separation from God as well as a metaphor for the celestial kingdom.[8] That tree, from which the sins of humanity hang as well as actual sinners, is ultimately accursed. The process of expiation for all of humanity passes through Adam's guilt and through the wood of the cross, as Saint Paul emphasizes in his Letter to the Galatians.[9] The wood of the tree is used to erect the cross of redemption, which washes the offense of the tree of Genesis,[10] but it is also used to build pagan idols.[11]

Among the intellectual tools with which the first missionaries landed in the Far East, the tree was conceptually important, which allows us to understand why one of them, the Portuguese Luís Fróis, paused with particular attention to observe the trees in those distant lands on the eastern edge of the world.[12] Endowed with an almost anthropological curiosity and capacity for observation, which would earn him the appreciation of Claude Lévi-Strauss centuries later, Fróis emphasized the distance in the manner of caring for and growing trees; but above all he recognized the almost sacred importance that the Japanese attributed to the cherry tree. Even today, every year, on the occasion of spring flowering, Japanese society is overcome by an almost maniacal, yet very primeval thrum of interest in the cherry tree and its flowers (*sakura*): that ancient tradition which required one to plant a cherry tree where a samurai was buried, so that the pure white of the *sakura* could be born from the red blood of the warrior.

In both Shinto and Buddhist culture, the tree plays a central role because it is considered the *axis mundi*, capable of connecting the underworld, the terrestrial world and the celestial world.[13] The symbolic correspondence of the tree in religious practices is the sacred pillar, which is planted in the ground to consecrate the surrounding space. The propagation of Buddhism in medieval Japan had occurred through the building of pillars, which were systematically uprooted by opponents. In ancient Japanese mythology, the conflict between old and new gods saw the woods and their trees as a battleground. Starting from the belief that the trunks were inhabited by spirits, the uprooting or felling of a tree meant driving away those deities, perhaps to make room for the construction of a Buddhist temple.[14] But after a period of rivalry and clash between Shinto and Buddhist cults, a sort of compromise had been reached, which had allowed a substantial cohabitation between the two and sanctioned the incorporation of the symbolic structure of the cult of the tree into the new Buddhist rites.[15]

The tree had thus assumed centrality even within the more complex new system of beliefs. Starting from the sacred trunks, craftsmen from Korea had begun to sculpt wooden images of the Buddha, which were then venerated by the local community. The sacred value was transmitted from the trunk to the image, with the result that these idols became animated objects capable of moving and expressing themselves independently, as well as performing miracles.[16] In the transition from Shintoism to Buddhism, ancient Japan witnessed a process of systematic substitution and superimposition: the Buddhist monks chose precisely those trunks, those trees, those natural places of worship around which older forms of worship had already developed.[17] In some cases, the diffusion of the new religion had passed through the inscription of sacred Buddhist images directly onto the trunks of previously venerated sacred trees, as happened systematically in the Nikko area, considered a divine land.[18] Ultimately, the branches taken from sacred trees and placed in homes became typical elements of Japanese religiosity, according to a logic shared by many other religions.[19]

Aware of the centrality of the tree in Japanese culture and of the pre-existence of substitution and overlapping mechanisms between different religions, the sixteenth-century missionaries of the Society of Jesus did not hesitate to play on the ambiguity between tree and cross to persuade those people considered by Francis Xavier on his arrival in Japan as "the best that have been discovered so far" to convert to the faith of a foreign God.[20] The sources used in these pages to reconstruct the overlap between trees and crosses are mostly internal sources of Ignatius of Loyola's order: chronicles, stories, but above all letters from the missionary fathers sent regularly from the Indies to the confreres who remained in Europe. It is therefore material to be used with caution, to the extent that its production corresponds to logics of persuasion and propaganda, and above all pursues the objective of promoting the Japanese mission in Europe, even before the need for a faithful account of the events. Like any product of travel literature, those texts oscillate continually between narration and information, and often it was the first pole, the more artificial one, that got the upper hand.[21] But their interest lies precisely in the fact that they inform us about the vision of the missionaries and about their way of interpreting the societies they are discovering, as well as giving an account of their own work in writing. Also, the stories about the miraculous trees in sixteenth- and seventeenth-century Japan allow us to observe the transformations and adjustments that the Counter-Reformation spirituality of the Jesuits went through in contact with another culture.

## The cross in the trunk

Since the first decades of the Christian presence in Japan, there had certainly been episodes of resistance to the strategies for conquering sacred space employed by the Jesuits. Bonzes and daimyos who remained faithful to the ancient faith had periodically encouraged the destruction of the great Christian crosses and persecuted the priests of Society, identified as deadly threats to traditional cults and the ancient gods.[22] Also aware that the conquest of souls passed through an appropriation of physical spaces, the Japanese hostile to the introduction of Christianity understood the importance of eradicating, from a material as well as a symbolic point of view, every presence of the new God who came from the sea. But as long as the Jesuits could count on the benevolent protection of Oda Nobunaga, the advance of the cross at the expense of pagodas and Buddhist idols did not stop. For example, during the 1570s, the daimyo Harunobu Arima (known in sources by the Christian name of Protasius), disavowed the choice to convert to Christianity at the death of his father, and at the instigation of the bonzes had the crosses uprooted and the priests expelled from his lands. After a few months he repented his choice and granted missionaries the "license to replace some of the uprooted crosses,"[23] then in 1579 personally embraced the Christian faith under the guidance of Valignano, becoming one of its most generous protectors.[24]

Shortly thereafter, however, in 1582, the unexpected death of Nobunaga and the rise of Hideyoshi significantly changed the balance. The Oda family had also built its power on a ruthless struggle against the powerful, rich and overly autonomous Buddhist monasteries, and he had therefore had every interest in reducing the cults connected to them, often with recourse to the use of force and with the parallel protection granted to the competing religion from the West. Whereas with Hideyoshi a new season was inaugurated.[25] After a few years – during which he preferred not to deviate too drastically from the line of his predecessor and seemed to continue to have a special eye for the Jesuits, continuing to surround himself with Christian lords such as Konishi

Yukinaga – in 1587, in the midst of the campaign for the conquest of Kyushu, Hideyoshi proclaimed the first ban of the priests of the Society and drove the feudal lords who had converted to Christianity into exile. Particularly notable was the ouster of Ukon Takayama, who had participated significantly in the campaign in the South.[26]

If Takayama preferred to renounce everything and start a new life consisting of exile and persecution, culminating in his exile to Manila in 1614, most of the converted lords chose to return to the ancient faith in order to preserve power, wealth and authority. On the cusp of the sixteenth and seventeenth centuries, the changed political conditions and the disappearance of those influential supports induced the Jesuits to rethink their expansion plans and, in particular, their somewhat too-visible policy of conquering sacred space. The time of expansion followed that of Nicodemitic withdrawal and accommodation. To continue to exist on Japanese soil, Christianity had to shed its skin, set aside the proud and vigorous spirit of its beginnings in favor of more cautious and prudent attitudes: crosses had to be hidden, churches had to give up their distinctive architectural character and adapt to the local style, so as to be less visible and more acceptable in the physical as well as mental landscape of Buddhist Japan. In this regard, the indications contained in *Il cerimoniale per i missionari del Giappone* edited by Valignano from 1585 onward to facilitate the integration of Christians into Japanese society are significant. Basically, by providing advice on the "way to build our houses and churches in Japan," the visitor called for maintaining the typical Western layout internally, but also adapting the rest to the forms suggested by the "good Japanese teachers." Only in this way – through a compromise, which was not always easy for those champions of Counter-Reformation Catholic conquest to accept – could the Christian faith continue to put down roots in the Land of the Rising Sun.[27]

Working against the Christians in Japan in the second half of the sixteenth century was also the excessive propensity of the priests, especially the Portuguese ones led by the mission superior Francisco Cabral, to get involved in the internal power games in the political life of the archipelago. Well established in commercial trade, the Jesuits acted as mediators with Lusitanian merchants and attempted to influence the daimyos closest to Christianity, prompting them to forge alliances with each other and wage war against feudal lords hostile to the new faith.[28] Such involvement could not find favor with Hideyoshi, intent on unifying the whole of Japan and subduing the powerful daimyos of the South. Despite the fact that contingents of Christian warriors were found among his own ranks, Hideyoshi began to distrust the autonomy of the lords converted to a foreign faith, too susceptible to those Western bonzes. The 1587 edict banning Christians, however, remained practically without consequences in the following years. The new ruler of the archipelago was satisfied with more prudent and submissive attitudes on the part of the Jesuit priests, and, in fact, still tolerated their cumbersome presence.

Forced to go on the defensive, the Society's change in strategy also had repercussions on the symbolic and spatial politics of the sacred. In the decades on the cusp of the sixteenth and seventeenth centuries, instead of erecting crosses, the line of accommodation promoted by Valignano led to the reinvestment of a Christian meaning in ancient forms and places of worship already exploited by the indigenous religions, not without this entailing a dose of ambiguity in the outcome.[29] Just as the early Church skillfully carried out a slow process of systematic replacement of pagan cults in the European countryside of the first centuries of the Christian era by superimposing the Virgin onto the Mother Goddess, and the saints – true and proper "arbiters of the sacred" – onto the various divinities of ancient agrarian religions,[30] so in late sixteenth-century Japan the Jesuits formulated similar penetration strategies, which had the undoubted privilege of attracting less attention from the authorities and being more seductive for the local population. But in spite of the first Christians, they moved with even greater caution. Whereas in the Old Continent the bishops of late ancient Gaul, Saint Martin and his disciples, did not hesitate to cut down the sacred trees of pagan cults to replace them with all-human sanctuaries and constructions,[31] the missionaries of the end of the sixteenth century did not limit themselves to preserving the functions of those ancient gods; rather, they wanted to preserve their trees and respect their natural cults, limiting themselves to reorienting them and incorporating them into a Christian perspective.[32] Symbolically, the age of trees followed the age of crosses.

As the Buddhist monks had already done before them, the Jesuits revived the ancient local cults, adapting them to the new faith. They resorted, for example, to the tree in sacred representations, directly inspired by traditional Japanese theater, with the clear aim of placing themselves in continuity with the initial religious context, to reconnect with the horizon of expectation, the sacred anticipation, the mythology and the cultic practices of the faithful.[33] Beginning in the 1590s, the story of a miraculous tree from the Omura region appeared in the correspondence of the missionaries, first mentioned in a letter from the Portuguese Jesuit Luís Fróis.[34] In the village of Obama, not far from the city of Arima, in Kyushu, on Christmas Eve, a Japanese Christian, a certain Leão, decided to send his son Miguel to collect wood.[35] Listless and eager to quickly fulfill his father's request, he came across a tree along the way. After almost a day's work, when evening fell, he preferred to return home empty-handed, promising himself to return at dawn the following day to finish the job.

As Fróis made sure to note, it was not just any tree, but a "Tara" – a tree all thorny on the outside and white inside, which

> is held in great veneration by the Gentiles because they believe it has a particular virtue against demons; for this reason, by placing it on the first day of the new year above the door of the house, they give themselves to

understand that they are safe from evil spirits, which very often give them trouble and strife.[36]

Specifically, the specimen chosen by Miguel was "very old, with no fruit, and almost completely dry."[37] Having returned on Christmas morning and resumed work, the young Christian, after dividing the trunk in two, saw "in the middle a very well made cross, more than half a palm long, of a color between red and black, the rest of the wood being very white, as it is naturally."[38] Struck by the miraculous event, Miguel ran to his father, in whose company he began to adore that divine sign. Two other Christians then took it upon themselves to deliver, the following day, the two pieces of trunk with engraved wooden crosses to the Jesuit priest who worked in the region and had come to say mass. During the celebration, the precious relic was placed by the priest on the altar and venerated as a "work of divine mercy that wanted such a sign to appear at that time."[39]

This was followed by the Jesuit clergy taking full possession and delivering the two crosses to the local superior in Arima, Pedro Gomez, and the initiation of an investigation procedure aimed at ascertaining the veracity of the miracle. The two wooden crosses were then placed inside a "gilded and well-made reliquary with glass so that they can be seen,"[40] initiating pilgrimages from the entire Japanese archipelago. However, the cult also extended to the exact place where the tree stood, from which the two chips with the crosses had been extracted: "here everyone made an effort to have as a relic a piece of the trunk, which had remained there, and for which cause not only was the wood taken away, but also the roots themselves, leaving almost nothing."[41]

Having become the fulcrum of "one of the most celebrated devotions in Japan,"[42] the holy wood attracted the attention of the above-mentioned Christian daimyo Harunobu Arima, who hastened to exploit the hierophany to strengthen his power and bond, which had been waning like his faith, with the priests of the Society. Fróis reported that, having learned of the miraculous cross, Harunobu rushed to come and venerate it and publicly recalled on the occasion that he had had a celestial vision in the previous months according to which "somewhere on his lands a sign of Jesus would be found, not made by human works."[43] Whether or not it was a ploy, the prophecy recalled by the daimyo had the direct consequence of inducing the priests to leave the precious relic on his lands, confirming that the logic of appropriation, both religious and political, were at play around the miraculous feat. Therefore, the hypothesis according to which, faced with a spontaneous popular cult based on previous pre-Christian models, the Jesuits promptly took possession of the hierophany to use it on a political level in order to strengthen the ever shaky faith of the local daimyo does not seem baseless. However, it was Harunobu/Protasius himself who provided the explanation of the event, proposing a double interpretation. "The manifestation of this cross in times of persecution," the Christian lord explained to the Jesuits, "seemed to him one of two things, either the holy cross and faith of Jesus Christ our savior should be embraced and revered throughout Japan, or the priests all had to die on the Cross."[44]

But beyond the prophetic sense attributed to it by the Jesuits and Protasius, there are other striking elements in the episode of the tree with the cross. As often happens in tales of miracles reworked by the Jesuits, and not only in the Far East, the story follows a predetermined plot: the discovery of the miraculous object – in this case the cross stamped into the trunk of the tree – i.e. the experience of hierophany, occurs through lay initiative; throughout the first part of the story the unveiling of the sacred is circumscribed within the natural world by the faithful, who, however, soon feel the need to turn to the ecclesiastical authorities, in this case to the nearest Jesuit, to announce the miraculous divine epiphany. Later, the priests took over, so to speak, physically taking possession of the relic and assuming full control of it, not without having verified, with a detailed investigation, the reliability of the witnesses' accounts and the effective truthfulness of the supernatural character of wooden crosses. Only the intervention of the priestly caste allows the metamorphosis of the piece of wood into a relic and fully legitimizes its immediate transformation into an object of worship. Finally, the seal of the priests produces the effect of making not only the discovery miraculous but also the crosses themselves, which from manifestations of the sacred become the very producers of the sacred.

## Christianizing ancient cults

The story of the miraculous tree of Arima presents another element of considerable interest, which concerns the relationship immediately established, in the words of the Jesuit priest, with the pre-Christian spiritual background. The tree in question, as mentioned, was not just any tree, but had already had its own previous sacral aspect within the local Shinto and Buddhist cults, and the fundamental characteristic of being able to drive out demons was recognized. For this reason, Fróis tells us, the Japanese would take branches at the beginning of the year to place inside their homes to protect the hearth.[45] And here the choice of the date of the story does not seem accidental: on December 25, a few days away from the celebration of the first of the year, that same tree revered by the Japanese underwent a transformation from a sacred pagan tree to a sacred Christian tree, coinciding with the nativity of Christ. Nevertheless, it did not lose its original characteristics in any way.

At the end of the story, in fact, some "effects" produced by the miraculous tree are presented, among which the story of a man who had lost his mind for over a year stands out. Having learned of the discovery of the crosses in the tree, his wife decided to go there, to remove a small piece from the trunk and make her mad husband drink it with water. The man immediately recovered his psychic stability. The fact of having ingested a piece of the sacred tree had the power to drive away the demon inhabiting his body.[46] In the account of the Jesuits, pieces of the sacred tree, ingested or placed at the entrance to the house, would retain the primordial protective and anti-demonic function attributed to them in the pre-Christian culture. It is proof, on the one hand, of a continuity of popular beliefs, despite the stratification of different doctrines, and on the other, above all, of the ability of the missionaries to appropriate and exploit previous cults and customs to bring the local populations closer to the Catholic faith.[47]

The Arima tree was not destined to remain an isolated case, as evidenced just two years later, in 1592, by the occurrence of a second episode that was similar in many ways, but which presented peculiar aspects worth examining. The worsening of persecutions against Christians and the now systematic dismantling of those crosses through which the Jesuits had deluded themselves that they could take over sacred Japanese spaces warranted a decisive change of context. The annual letter from Japan was once again written by Father Fróis, who, however, in this second case, was more explicit in emphasizing the existence of a link between the destruction of the wooden crosses by the authorities and the appearance of a miraculous new cross on the trunk of a tree.[48] The episode took place in the castle of Fukuda ("Fucunda"), in the lands of Ōmura, governed by a Christian lord, Dom Sancho (Yoshiaki), and was explicitly interpreted as a recurrence of the miracle of Arima.[49] On February 7, 1592, a Friday, the day of the Passion of Christ, Mathias, a Christian residing at the local church, decided to have his son Simão cut down a tree called "caquinoqui" by the Japanese, a very common tree producing round apple-like fruits and resistant over time, like the fig tree.[50] This tree, however, hadn't produced any fruit for two years. Simão set to work, but in splitting the trunk, "four crosses were discovered on both sides of the wood, […] and they were black, the rest of the tree being very white."[51]

As had happened in Arima, word of the miraculous trunk began spread, attracting a growing number of faithful, and prompting the laity to turn to the Jesuit priest of the region. Warned in turn, Valignano initiated a "diligent investigation of this event," receiving confirmation "that everything is true in accordance with what has been said."[52] Unlike the previous case, here the Jesuits were more cautious in exhibiting the new relic so as not to attract the attention of the central authorities hostile to Christianity. "In order not to give rise to rumors and to discourage the gathering of people"[53] it was decided to keep those crosses in a decent place and to reserve them solely for the sight of Portuguese and local Christian nobles – including, naturally, Dom Sancho and his knights – honored by that divine gift manifested right on their lands. The sacred trunks were placed in a reliquary and safeguarded until, once the persecutions passed, it would be possible to publicly honor them, rendering them the due solemnity.

## 56  The miraculous tree

A change in atmosphere could be detected, with a pervading feeling of insecurity that ended up influencing the very cult of the relic, available but not fully usable by the Christian community. In an age when pagan persecutors were destroying crosses, God himself intervened by revealing the existence of new crosses within the natural world, hidden in the trunks of trees but within the reach of his faithful. That Christian God who had appeared invincible and triumphant in the first decades of the Jesuit presence in the Far East now showed his hidden face: he was able to hide behind the appearances of the natural world and reveal himself in a discreet way to those who had faith, without arousing scandal among his persecutors. Together with him, the Japanese Christian community as a whole took a simulating, Nicodemitic approach. Fróis conveyed the idea well through a further metaphor, when he compared the Christians of Japan to a ship in a storm: tossed by the waves of the sea, it is capable of submerging the bow under water and then resurfacing with the help of the holy cross.[54]

Both in Arima and in Omura – two of the Christian lands par excellence in samurai Japan – a precise correspondence emerged between pre-Christian cultic customs and acts of devotion linked to the wooden crosses discovered in the trunks of trees. In all probability, on their own initiative, Japanese Christians approached the Christian sacred tree just as their ancestors had approached the Shinto or Buddhist sacred trees for centuries if not millennia. In addition to coming to venerate the crosses, they would appropriate pieces of the trunk or even the remains of the cut tree, and even its roots. They would make a particular use of those pieces of the sacred relic: on the one hand they place them at the entrance of the houses to drive out demons; on the other, they consumed them with water to directly benefit from the incorporated and digested holiness. Such behavior follows in form what occurred in various religious contexts, and in ancient Japan itself, when the sacred object revealed itself as a powerful producer of holiness, which it emanates and spreads throughout the surrounding space.[55]

Even more impressive is the correspondence between the Jesuit story of the cross depicted in the trunk of the tree and ancient Buddhist legends in which images of the Buddha are inscribed on the wood of the Japanese trunks. For example, in one of these it is said that a man from the district of Muza, during the reign of Emperor Shōmu (724-749 AD), who went to the mountains to pray among the trees, came across a horse chestnut whose trunk had been cut to extract wooden statues of the Buddha before being abandoned on the ground. One of the trunks served as a bridge for men and animals to cross the river. Just as he crossed it, the man heard a voice begging him not to walk on it. It was the animated trunk that demanded that the work be finished and an image of the Buddha carved inside it, as in fact the traveler then undertook to do.[56] In another miraculous tale, set in the Ama district, while collecting firewood, a boy carved an image of the Buddha in a piece of wood which he then placed in a pagoda in the rock, starting a cult. Sometime later, an ignorant man stumbled across the wooden statue carved by the boy and broke it. He was immediately struck by divine fury, started bleeding from his nose and mouth, collapsed to the ground and died.[57] But beyond the specific case of the sacred image carved into the trunks, there are numerous examples that can be drawn from the ancient Buddhist legends of wooden statues that perform miracles, interrupt the execution of a condemned man,[58] restore sight to a woman blind,[59] move to flee fires,[60] hide in the sand,[61] or become irritated by ant bites.[62]

Precisely because it was grafted onto a previous cultic ground and could therefore make use of a millenary inclination of the local population for the veneration of images carved into trunks,[63] the miraculous Christian tree reappeared in Jesuit writings almost until the end of their presence in Japan and thus accompanied the entire course of the Christian century in the Land of the Rising Sun. On the eve of the almost definitive expulsion of the priests from the Japanese archipelago, in the autumn of 1614, there was a second epidemic of crosses in the trunks, as attested by the correspondence of the last Jesuits remaining on Japanese soil. At the bottom of the 1611 annual letter, written from Nagasaki, João Rodrigues Giram reports yet another episode of a miraculous trunk, which seems to trace, almost down to the smallest detail, the stories of over twenty years earlier. In Cori, a village in the lands of Vomurandono, a neophyte Christian by the name of Fabian had in the garden of a villa a tree which the Japanese call "caquinoqui" – the same one already encountered in Omura and similar to the European fig tree: with a very hard trunk and producing soft fruits that can be stored for a long time, once dried.[64]

As in the previous episodes, Fabian's specimen had not produced fruit for two years, and for this reason it was decided to cut it and let it dry on the ground. After several months, Fabian returned to the trunk and noticed the appearance of "a black cross in one of those chips, the trunk being white."[65] Calling his son Paulo, he could only ascertain that it was a matter of a supernatural and miraculous intervention. He then decided to keep the sacred relic secretly, since "it did not seem the right time to reveal it, but perhaps a day would come when it would surely be discovered."[66] The neophyte's prudence attested to a climate of intolerance and persecution, which in fact corresponded to the years 1610 and 1611, when the new ruler of Japan, Ieyasu Tokugawa, had chosen to definitively rid the land of the cumbersome Jesuit presence.

As if in a theatrical plot, despite the Nicodemitic prudence of the discoverer, the episode reached the ears of other Christians who flocked to the site of the hierophany. A first miracle even took place: another neophyte, suffering from quartan fever, went to where the tree had been severed, took a small piece of wood, mixed it with water and ingested it, upon which he was miraculously healed.[67] But even in Cori, the laity's importance soon gave way. Some faithful, "considering it unreasonable that such sacred things should be kept in the home of a layman," warned a Jesuit priest, who sent one of his colleagues to verify the situation.[68] Despite the resistance of Fabian, who feared for his own safety and preferred to have the cross remain hidden in his house so as not to arouse the ire of the local pagan lord, the local devotion ended up growing all the same and even important figures of the local aristocracy were allowed to venerate the relic. But in addition to the trunk with the cross, it was the entire original tree that experienced growing success.[69]

The overlapping dynamics between the new Christian cult and the older rites of incorporating the sacred object by chewing pieces of the trunk was therefore re-proposed.[70] Miracles of healings and exorcisms followed one another: a man who for years had had his home troubled by demonic spirits obtained permission from Fabian to be able to place the cross within his walls for one night; in the morning the house was freed from the demonic presence.[71] Here too the thaumaturgical and protective power of sacred wood echoes, which, like the branches placed at the entrance, was able to drive away spirits. The ability of the Christian God to superimpose over ancient "pagan" beliefs, or in any case to draw inspiration directly from them, made those miracles convincing not only in the eyes of the Christians themselves, but also of the "gentiles," struck by the power of the new God.[72] The aim was therefore achieved: the recovery of traditional practices and their Christianization had the effect of attracting new followers to the faith of the Padres as well as triggering further discoveries of miraculous crosses.[73]

Two years later, in 1613, the interpretation of events changed: faced with yet another apparition of a miraculous fig tree, the Jesuit priest in charge of drafting the annual letter immediately pointed out that the "sign of the most holy cross" found while "cutting down a fig tree" was a consolation sent by the Lord to gird up "these Christians to future persecution."[74] The cross in the tree, therefore, became not just a sign of divine intervention, but above all a prefiguration and warning of the imminent martyrdom of the priests, persecuted and crucified for their faith. Moreover, the whole episode was characterized by disturbing aspects for the faithful who, after having discovered the miraculous trunk, were forced by the local lord to redeem it by giving up all their possessions, abandoning their land, and taking refuge with the precious relic in Nagasaki, the last bastion of the Christian faith in Japan.[75] From the preceding story it is evident that by this time, on the eve of the expulsion of the priests from the Japanese archipelago, the cross in the tree was interpreted more as a dramatic omen of death and martyrdom; it no longer evoked the triumphant standard of a conquering Catholicism, but rather the crosses of the Passion.[76] From the time of the tree we return to the time of the crosses, according to an interpretation then duly taken up by later Jesuit authors, including the Portuguese Luis Piñeiro, author in 1617 of a *Relacíon del suceso que tuvo nuestra santa fe en los Reinos del Japón, desde el año de seiscientos y doce hasta el de seiscientos y quince*.[77]

In conclusion, it must be remembered that the stories of miraculous statues and images capable of healing the faithful, as well as of hiding, moving, being saved from persecution, and triggering conversions in the surrounding space, were not exclusive to the missionaries in the Far East. On the contrary, these are narratives that correspond to a very specific discursive framework, which recur in Jesuit writings and which were also widely exploited in other geographical and political contexts. The most evident testimony comes from a collective work of the entire Jesuit order, whose editing and publication was done by the Bavarian priest Wilhelm Gumppenberg in the mid-seventeenth century. In the aftermath of the Thirty Years' War, between 1657 and 1659, the first version in German and Latin of the *Atlas Marianus* was published, an encyclopedic work elaborated over almost twenty years, which brought together around a hundred stories relating to Marian shrines, located mostly in Europe, in the Habsburg territories, with three Latin American exceptions always in areas dominated by the Spanish monarchy.[78]

A vast catalog of sacred images of the Virgin and short stories on the origin of the cult of each of them, the work is hard to classify, to the extent that it is not a mere collection of miracles, nor a guide for pilgrimages, nor a dogmatic treatise, but rather it belongs to the genre of "sacred topographies."[79] Beyond the theoretical definitions, the *Atlas* reveals itself to be, above all, a manifesto of Counter-Reformation Catholicism, for the enhancement of the figure of Mary, protector of the Catholic armies against pagans and heretics, of her mediating function between heaven and earth, and of the role of the miracle, as well as the attention it brought to the geography of confessional barriers. Right from the title page, in which the Virgin is seated on the roof of the Holy House of Loreto – suspended between heaven and earth, illuminating the world that has remained Catholic, leaving the Protestant lands in semi-darkness – the work is distinguished by its planetary projection characteristic of the Jesuit order and is configured as an attempt to give life to a Catholic cosmography, albeit with an obvious preference for sanctuaries managed or attributable to the Society rather than to other orders.[80]

From those founding stories emerged a religiosity populated by anthropomorphic images that took on a precise identity, with a name, a history, a memory, a body and desires. There were also thaumaturgical and miraculous objects which, having retained part of the saving power of the Virgin, revealed themselves capable of healing the sick and exerting a supernatural action on events. Even when it came to a miraculous tree – as in the case of the foundation story relating to a sanctuary in Ravenna – the association was made with the image of the Virgin hanging from its branches, which had the supernatural power to cure the faithful who had come to worship her and defend the city from a terrible flood.[81] So compared to the Japanese trees of the missionary letters from the Far East, at the heart of the narrative device of Gumppenberg and his correspondents, only the cult of the Virgin was systematically treated, in a clearly controversial and polemical function with respect to the Protestant world. Significantly, neither in the first reduced version nor in the much more extensive one, released in 1672 and including 1,200 sanctuaries from Mexico to India,[82] do sanctuaries and stories inspired by the Japanese mission appear, where the cult of the cross was preferred to the cult of the Virgin.

The parallel with the *Atlas*, which enjoyed undoubted success in seventeenth-century Europe and was then reprinted in the following centuries up to the nineteenth, therefore, allows us to appreciate the peculiarity and originality of Japanese Christianity as elaborated by Jesuit missionaries between the sixteenth and seventeenth centuries – even compared to its European and South American brethren. It also demonstrates the variety of ways the Society took in interpreting and developing strategies for the conquest of souls and space in non-European territories.

## Notes

1. Tronu Montane, *Sacred Space and Ritual in Early Modern Japan*, cit., pp. 72–74.
2. Morishita, *L'art des missions catholiques au Japon (XVI<sup>e</sup>–XVII<sup>e</sup> siècle)*, cit., pp. 53–55, 267; Silvia Vesco, *L'arte giapponese dalle origini all'età moderna*, Torino, Einaudi, 2021, pp. 416–17.
3. A similar flexibility on the part of the Jesuits in seeking concepts within Buddhist culture capable of acting as bridges is found with the translations of some Western texts into Japanese, as well as in the re-use of pictorial techniques of the local tradition (Ivi, pp. 202–3).
4. See the entry "Trees," in *Encyclopedia of Religion (Second Edition)*, ed. Lindsay Jones, Detroit, Thomson Gale, 2005, vol. 14, pp. 9333–40; Mircea Eliade, *The Sacred and the Profane. The Nature of Religion*, New York, Harper and Brothers, 1961 (1957), pp. 147–51; Id., *Traité d'histoire des religions*, cit., pp. 232–84; Ries, *Simbolo. Le costanti del sacro*, cit., pp. 131–33.
5. Giulio Busi, *Simboli del pensiero ebraico*, Torino, Einaudi, 1999, p. 55.
6. Stephen Greenblatt, *The Rise and Fall of Adam and Eve*, New York and London, W. W. Norton and Company, 2017; Guillaume Alonge, Olivier Christin, *Adam et Ève, le paradis, la viande et les légumes*, Toulouse, Anacharsis, 2023.
7. Ries, *Simbolo. Le costanti del sacro*, cit., pp. 162–63.
8. "He went on to say, 'What is the kingdom of God like? What shall I compare it with? It is like a mustard seed which a man took and threw into his garden: it grew and became a tree, and the birds of the air sheltered in its branches.'" (Jerusalem Bible: Luke 13:18–19).
9. "Christ redeemed us from the curse of the Law by being cursed for our sake, since scripture says: Cursed be everyone who is hanged on a tree! This was done so that in Christ Jesus the blessing of Abraham might include the pagans, and so that through faith we might receive the promised Spirit." (Jerusalem Bible: Gal. 3:13–14). Bart D. Ehrman, *The Triumph of Christianity: How a Forbidden Religion Swept the World*, London, Oneworld, 2019 (2018), p. 53. For the different exegetical meanings of the term ξύλον (wood, cross, tree…) cf. *Dizionario esegetico del Nuovo Testamento*, ed. Horst Balz, Gerhard Schneider, Brescia, Paideia, 2004, pp. 534–36.
10. Eliade, *Traité d'histoire des religions*, cit., pp. 253–55.
11. Ehrman, *The Triumph of Christianity*, cit., pp. 66–67.
12. Luis Fróis, *Européens et Japonais. Traité sur les contradictions et différences de mœurs*, Paris, Chandeigne, 2015, p. 75; Castel-Branco, Carvalho, *Luis Fróis: First Western Accounts of Japan's Gardens, Cities and Landscapes*, cit., pp. 199–222.

## The miraculous tree 61

More generally on the description of gardens and plants inside Japanese sanctuaries by the Jesuit priests, cf. ivi, pp. 59–155.
13 Kyoko M. Nakamura, *La sacralità dell'albero nella letteratura popolare buddhista*, in *Giappone. Grandi religioni e culture nell'Estremo Oriente*, a cura di Lawrence E. Sullivan (ed. it. a cura di Paolo Villani), Milano, Jaca Book, 2006, pp. 251–63.
14 For an insightful reflection on the role of the tree in ancient Japanese culture see Fabio Rambelli, *Buddhist Materiality. A Cultural History of Objects in Japanese Buddhism*, Stanford, Stanford University Press, 2007, pp. 129–71.
15 Nakamura, *La sacralità dell'albero nella letteratura popolare buddhista*, cit., p. 262.
16 Ivi, pp. 258–59.
17 Fabietti, *Materia sacra*, cit., pp. 205–7.
18 Nakamura, *La sacralità dell'albero nella letteratura popolare buddhista*, cit., p. 260.
19 Exemplified by the materials exposed by James George Frazer, *The Golden Bough. A New Abridgement from the Second and Third Editions*, edited with an introduction and notes by Robert Fraser, Oxford, Oxford University Press, 2009, pp. 82–97; Id., *Il ramo d'oro. Studio sulla magia e la religione*, Torino, Bollati Boringhieri, 2019, pp. 137–66. See also for the Japanese case Mircea Eliade (ed.), *Dizionario delle religioni dell'Estremo Oriente*, Milano, Jaca Book, 2020, pp. 544–48.
20 Francis Xavier to fellow residents in Goa, Kagoshima, November 5, 1549, in *Avisi particolari dalle Indie di Portogallo*, Roma, Valerio Dorico e Luigi Fratelli Bressani, 1552, p. 288; for a recent edition Xavier, *Epistolae S. Francisci Xaverii aliaque eius scripta*, cit., vol. 2: 1549–52, p. 186. A careful analysis of the overlap between the cult of trees and the cult of the cross can already be found in the beautiful volume by Giovanni Isgrò, *L'avventura scenica dei gesuiti in Giappone*, Bari, Edizioni di pagina, 2016, pp. 13–14, 88–93.
21 Sergio Bozzola, *Retorica e narrazione del viaggio. Diari, relazioni, itinerari fra Quattro e Cinquecento*, Roma, Salerno Editrice, 2020, pp. 72–109.
22 For example for the Bungo region cf. Bartoli, *Dell'Historia della Compagnia*, cit., pp. 278, 697.
23 Ivi, p. 97.
24 Steichen, *Les daimyō chrétiens*, cit., pp. 116–17. Boxer, *The Christian Century in Japan, 1549–1650*, cit., pp. 138, 270–85, 314–15; George Elison, *Deus Destroyed. The Image of Christianity in Early Modern Japan*, Cambridge-London, Harvard University Press, 1988, pp. 28, 64. Alessandro Valignano also dedicates a paragraph to Harunobu in his *Sumario* (Valignano, *Sumario de las cosas de Japon (1583)*, cit., pp. 82–91).
25 Ninomiya, *Le Japon pré-moderne, 1573-1867*, cit., pp. 46–48.
26 Cf. *supra* chap. 1 and *infra* chap. 5.
27 Alexandro Valignano, *Il cerimoniale per i missionari del Giappone*, ed. Josef Franz Schütte, Michela Catto, Roma, Edizioni di storia e letteratura, 2011, pp. 270–81.
28 Boxer, *The Christian Century in Japan, 1549-1650*, cit., pp. 145–49.
29 "L'accueil empressé faits aux véroniques et aux Agnus dei révèle une étonnante convergence entre les pratiques populaires européennes et japonaises. Les vertus apotropaïques attachées à ces objets bénis par les papes ont facilité le transfert d'une religion à l'autre sans que les missionnaires, trop enclins à voir des explications surnaturelles, aient compris l'ambiguïté sous-jacente à l'empressement des Japonais" (Morishita, *L'art des missions catholiques au Japon (XVI$^e$–XVII$^e$ siècle)*, cit., p. 224).

30 Peter Brown, *Authority and the Sacred. Aspects of the Christianisation of the Roman World*, Cambridge, Cambridge University Press, 1995, pp. 57–78; Ewa Wipszycka, *Storia della Chiesa nella tarda antichità*, Milano, Mondadori, 2000, pp. 317–19; Chris Wickham, *The Inheritance of Rome. A History of Europe from 400 to 1000*, London, Allen Lane, 2009, pp. 54–58.
31 Ehrman, *The Triumph of Christianity*, cit., pp. 150–51.
32 Peter Brown, *The Cult of the Saints. Its Rise and Function in Latin Christianity*, Chicago, The University of Chicago Press, 1981, pp. 124–27; Ucerler, *The Samurai and the Cross*, cit., pp. 56–62.
33 Isgrò, *L'avventura scenica dei gesuiti in Giappone*, cit., pp. 65–66.
34 The episode is then taken up by various other authors of the Society: as well as by Bartoli in the seventeenth century and by Charlevoix in the eighteenth century (Pierre-François-Xavier de Charlevoix, *Histoire de l'établissement des progrès et de la décadence du Christianisme dans l'empire du Japon*, Rouen, Guillaume Behourt, 1715, III, pp. 55–58), who limit themselves to faithfully reproducing the story of the missionaries, the miraculous Japanese trees are mentioned by Wilhelm Gumppenberg in his *Atlas Marianus*, a large collection of stories about miraculous images. See Nicolas Balzamo, Olivier Christin, Fabrice Flückiger (ed.), *L'Atlas Marianus de Wilhelm Gumppenberg. Édition et traduction*, Neuchâtel, Editions Alphil-Presses universitaires suisses, 2015, p. 434.
35 *Copia di due lettere annue scritte dal Giapone del 1589 e 1590...*, Roma, Luigi Zannetti, 1593, pp. 68–77. The episode then picked up in Fróis, *Historia de Japam*, cit., V, pp. 201–8.
36 "da' gentili è havuto in grande veneratione perché tengono che habbia particolar virtù contra i demoni; per il che mettendolo il primo giorno dell'anno nuovo sopra la porta della casa, si danno ad intendere esser sicuri da spiriti maligni, che ben spesso danno loro molestia e travaglio" (*Copia di due lettere annue scritte dal Giapone del 1589 e 1590*, cit., p. 68).
37 "molto vecchio, e di niun frutto, e quasi del tutto secco" (Ivi, p. 68).
38 "nel mezzo una croce molto ben fatta, lunga più di mezzo palmo, di colore tra rosso e nero, essendo il restante del legno molto bianco, come è naturalmente" (Ivi, p. 69).
39 "opera della divina misericordia, che haveva voluto che apparisse in quel tempo un segno tale" (Ivi, p. 70).
40 "reliquiario dorato e ben fatto con vetri acciò si possino vedere" (Ivi, p. 70).
41 "quivi ciascuno faceva tutto il suo sforzo per havere per reliquia un pezzetto del tronco, che vi era restato, per la qual causa non solo portorno via quanto vi era del legno, ma anche le radici stesse, non lasciando quasi niente" (Ivi, p. 71).
42 "una delle più celebri devotioni che siano nel Giappone" (Ivi, p. 71).
43 "in un luogho delle sue terre si sarebbe trovato un segno di Giesù, non fatto per opra humana" (Ivi, p. 72).
44 "Il manifestarsi questa croce in tempo di persecutione [...] gli pareva che una delle due cose, o che la santa croce, et fede di Giesù Christo salvator nostro doveva esser abbracciata, et riverita in tutto il Giapone, o vero che li padri havevano tutti da morire in Croce" (Ivi, p. 73).
45 The missionaries questioned whether it would be permissible to allow converts to continue decorating their homes with twigs on Buddhist holidays (Proust, *L'Europe au prisme du Japon*, cit., pp. 111–12).
46 In many ways the subsequent story of a possessed woman freed from contact with the cross is similar.
47 Fabietti, *Materia sacra*, cit., pp. 171–76.
48 *Lettera del Giapone degli anni 1591 et 1592...*, Roma, Luigi Zannetti, 1595, p. 135.
49 Ivi, pp. 135–39. Cf. also Fróis, *Historia de Japam*, cit., V, pp. 389–99.

50 In addition to reasons of purely physical similarity, the comparison with the European fig proposed by the fathers is functional in establishing a link with the evangelical passage of the dried fig that bears no fruit (Luke 13:6–9).
51 "dall'una e dall'altra parte del legno si scoprirono quattro croci, [...] et erano di color nero, essendo il resto dell'albero molto bianco" (*Lettera del Giapone degli anni 1591 et 1592*, cit., p. 136).
52 "diligente inquisitione di questo fatto [...] il tutto esser vero conforme a quanto s'è detto" (Ivi, p. 137).
53 "Per non dar luogo a romori, e per schifare il concorso della gente" (Ivi, p. 137).
54 Ivi, p. 138.
55 Eliade, *Traité d'histoire des religions*, cit., pp. 265–66.
56 *Miraculous Stories from the Japanese Buddhist Tradition. The Nihon ryoiki of the Monk Kyokai*, ed. Kyoko Motomochi Nakamura, London-New York, Routledge, 2014, p. 196.
57 Ivi, pp. 262–63.
58 Ivi, pp. 231–32.
59 Ivi, pp. 236–37.
60 Ivi, p. 210.
61 Ivi, pp. 211–12.
62 Ivi, pp. 261–62.
63 Rambelli, *Buddhist Materiality*, cit., pp. 141–53.
64 *Lettera annua del Giappone del MDCXI al molto reverendo padre Claudio Acquaviva, generale della Compagnia di Giesù...*, Roma, Bartolomeo Zannetti, 1615, pp. 111–17.
65 "in una di quelle schegge una croce di color negro, essendo il tronco bianco" (Ivi, p. 112).
66 "all'hora non gli pareva tempo di palesarla, ma sarebbe forse venuto un giorno che l'haverebbono scoperta sicuramente" (Ivi, p. 112).
67 Ivi, pp. 113–14. It is worth emphasizing that in the biblical culture in which the missionaries were seeped, the fig tree already possessed healing qualities (Busi, *Simboli del pensiero ebraico*, cit., p. 51).
68 "non parendogli ragionevole che cosa sì sacra si conservasse in casa d'un laico" (*Lettera annua del Giappone del MDCXI*, cit., p. 114).
69 "Si cominciò a far gran conto dell'istesso tronco dove fu ritrovata, massime quando s'intese che molti havendo preso di quel legno e sminuzzatolo, e posto in acqua, della quale poi bevendo s'erano miracolosamente liberati da febbre terzana, e quartana, onde quelli che non potevano havere qualche pezzetto di quella schieggia dove era la croce, si rivoltorno a prendere qualche poco del tronco, il quale ancora stavasi in terra, nel luogo dove fu reciso, e tagliato in pezzi, in brevissimo tempo lo portorno via tutto, anzi si diedero ancora a cavare le radici di quell'albero, tanto fu la devotione di quei neofiti: ne è meraviglia, perché l'istessi gentili ne fecero grandissimo conto, come di cosa miracolosa, e più restorno confermati da un gran miracolo che poco dopo seguì" (ivi, pp. 115–16).
70 Years later, on the occasion of the collection of testimonies for the cause of beatification of the 26 Martyrs of Nagasaki, one of the miracles following the martyrdom was the case of an indigenous woman who, on the verge of death, suddenly recovered after ingesting a piece of the cross on which the Franciscan Bautista was martyred (Omata Rappo, *Des indes lointaines aux scènes des collèges*, cit., p. 155).
71 *Lettera annua del Giappone del MDCXI*, cit., p. 116.
72 Also in this circumstance there is no lack of clerical control over the event, with the "*diligente informatione*" promoted by the bishop of Japan (ivi).
73 On the cross discovered by a woodcutter in the countryside surrounding Nagasaki cf. ivi, pp. 117–19.

74 "segno della santissima croce [...] tagliando un albero di fico [...] questi christiani alla futura persecutione" (*Lettera annua del Giappone dell'anno M.DC.XIII. nella quale si raccontano molte cose d'edificatione, e martirii occorsi nella persecutione di questo anno*, Roma, Bartolomeo Zannetti, 1617, p. 10).

75 Ivi, pp. 10–11.

76 Moreover, it was precisely the prefiguration of martyrdom that the seventeenth-century Jesuit historians Daniello Bartoli and Nicolas Trigault wanted to give to these prodigious crosses (Bartoli, *Dell'Historia della Compagnia*, cit., pp. 418, 659–63; Trigault, *Histoire des martyrs du Japon depuis l'an MDCXII jusqu'à MDCXX*, Paris, Sebastien Cramoisy, 1624, p. 14). On such an interpretation cf. Omata Rappo, *Des indes lointaines aux scènes des collèges*, cit., pp. 345–51.

77 "Lo que nuestro Señor pretendio en el aparecimiento desta cruzes no lo sabemos: lo que se sabe es, que despues de halladas se seguio la persecucion, en que huvo cruzificados, degollados, quemados, y muchos otros generos de martirios: pero como la santa Cruz de Christo nuestro Señor, no solo sea señal de trabajo, sino tambien de vitoria, podemos confiar en su divina virtud, que pues al aparecimiento se siguio la persecucion de que tratamos, trasella se sseguiria el triunfo que esperamos" (Piñeiro, *Relacíon del suceso que tuvo nuestra santa fe en los Reinos del Japón*, cit., pp. 5–12, especially p. 12). Cf. Rady Roldán-Figueroa, *The Martyrs of Japan. Publication History and Catholic Missions in the Spanish World (Spain, New Spain, and the Philippines, 1597–1700)*, Leiden-Boston, Brill, 2021, pp. 211–12.

78 For a recent critical edition cf. Balzamo, Christin, Flückiger (ed.), *L'Atlas Marianus de Wilhelm Gumppenberg*. Édition et traduction, cit.

79 Dominique Julia, *Sanctuaires et lieux sacrés à l'époque moderne*, in André Vauchez (ed.), *Lieux sacrés lieux de cultes, sanctuaires*, Roma, École française de Rome, 2000, pp. 257–63.

80 Olivier Christin, Fabrice Flückiger, *L'Atlas Marianus de Wilhelm Gumppenberg: une topographie sacrée à l'âge de la science classique*, in Olivier Christin, Fabrice Flückiger, Naïma Ghermani (ed.), *Marie mondialisée. L'Atlas Marianus de Wilhelm Gumppenberg et les topographies sacrées de l'époque moderne*, Neuchâtel, Éditions Alphil-Presses universitaires suisses, 2014, pp. 9–23.

81 Balzamo, Christin, Flückiger (ed.), *L'Atlas Marianus de Wilhelm Gumppenberg. Édition et traduction*, cit., pp. 192–94.

82 Wilhelm Gumppenberg, *Atlas marianus quo Sanctae Dei genitricis Mariae imaginum miraculosarum origines duodecim historiarum centuriis explicantur*, Monachii, Ioannis Iaeckini, 1672, 2 voll.

# 4 The wood of martyrdom

## Crosses of blood

When crosses appeared in the trunks of trees in Cori and Nagasaki in 1611, the age of compromise and hiding, of a faith disguised but in fact still tolerated by the Japanese authorities, was drawing to a close in the Empire of the Rising Sun. By then, in that promised land which had suddenly turned into a hell of persecution, none of the remaining priests had the illusion that the signs sent from heaven could prefigure a radiant future for the faith of Christ, let alone be the harbinger of the entire archipelago's approaching conversion. Abraham's God had expressed himself unambiguously, all that remained for his faithful was to become aware of it: the crosses hidden in the trees were nothing more than the omen of the imminent martyrdom that awaited Japanese Christians and Western missionaries. At this point, the crosses in the trunks gave way to the real crosses, planted on the heights of Nagasaki, as had already happened in 1597. The Jesuit missionaries, for their part, had been trained and prepared for martyrdom since their entry as young men into European colleges. Martyrdom had been their spiritual horizon, their authentic vocation as they eagerly left for the Indies, to discover very distant and unexplored lands as well as pagan peoples to rescue and convert. But above all they were eager to shed their blood for the sake of spreading their faith.[1] Obedient soldiers of Christ, fanatics of God, aspiring saints ready for extreme torture,[2] but also restless souls as protagonists in a personal journey of purification and spiritual asceticism;[3] the missionaries in their writings never cease to invoke the desire to die on the cross for a fuller identification with the Christ of the Passion.[4]

For some of them, Golgotha assumed the name of Tateyama, the hill just outside Nagasaki, on which, in February 1597, the Japanese authorities erected 26 crosses intended for the torture of Christians,[5] whose corpses remained exposed for months. Indeed, during his world tour, the Florentine merchant and traveler Francesco Carletti was still able to contemplate the horrendous spectacle of decomposing bodies when he landed there in June of the same year.[6] But how did that sudden acceleration in the persecution by the Japanese authorities come about? How did the cautious Nicodemitic strategy adopted by the Jesuits in the previous decade backfire to the point of attracting the

DOI: 10.4324/9781003275008-5

violent repression of the central power at the end of Hideyoshi's rule? One of the main exponents of the Jesuit mission in the Far East, Luís Fróis, attempted to offer an articulated answer to these questions, which raised doubts about the very meaning of the missionary effort. He chose to dedicate a slim book to the painful story of the 26 martyrs of Nagasaki intended for the European public. In those pages, in addition to retracing the main stages of martyrdom, he questioned the shift made by the authorities and gave an account of the Society's work, identifying the origin of the change in atmosphere since the arrival in Japan of the Franciscan priests.[7] But Fróis was not the only one to tackle the argument, as demonstrated by another contemporary work written by the Franciscan Juan de Santa María, which proposed keys to different if not opposite readings.[8]

The existence of a double memory of the tragic episode – Jesuit and Franciscan – shows that at the end of the century the Jesuits were no longer alone and had by now lost the monopoly of evangelization in the Japanese archipelago, forced to deal with the uncomfortable competition of the discalced Franciscans.[9] If in the Americas the first missionaries had been the Franciscans and Dominicans, only later joined by the disciples of Ignatius, who managed in their Paraguayan *reducciones* to set up a different type of evangelization of indigenous peoples,[10] the exact opposite happened in Japan. Starting in the 1590s, the accommodating style of the Jesuits had to contend with that of the mendicant orders, linked to more traditional conversion strategies. Superimposed over the rivalry between alternative missionary styles was the political competition due to the protection of the respective orders. Since Francis Xavier's first trips to the East, the Society of Jesus had obtained financial as well as logistical support from the Portuguese crown, while the Franciscans had followed in the footsteps of the Spanish conquistadors, who settled in the Philippines. The union between the two crowns in 1581, under Philip II, favored the Franciscan ambitions of penetrating the Japanese archipelago, traditionally exclusive to the Jesuits/Portuguese.

Reading between the lines – but not too far in between – of Fróis and Juan de Santa María's pages, a rivalry emerged between the two missionary orders, sparked from the first months of cohabitation, as they were forced to contend for the conversion of Japanese souls. And they were ready to argue with each other on a global scale, with exchanges of poisonous accusations and insinuations.[11] The approaches appeared to be diametrically opposed: the Franciscans exalted the martyrological dimension of their adventurous landing in Japan, following the representatives of the king of Spain, sent by the governor of the Philippines.[12] Similar to how it had been for the first Jesuits, the activity of the followers of the Saint Francis was driven by an eagerness to convert and public preach the true faith, without any regard for local religious and political balances, in defiance of the warnings and threats from the Japanese authorities. The path to martyrdom cut through the daily actions of the Franciscan missionaries almost naturally; they founded churches, preached in public, and inevitably wound up attracting the ire of Hideyoshi.

In the Franciscan report there is no shortage of criticism with respect to the work of the Jesuits, who were certainly credited with being the first to establish Christian roots in that foreign land, but also stigmatized for excessive caution, Nicodemitic prudence, lack of humility, envy, and effectively the failure to bring the explosive message of the Gospel to fruition among the pagans.[13] The burden and honor of relaunching the evangelization of those lands, therefore, fell to the Franciscans and not to others, as they were the only authentic guardians of the true faith.[14] And the Franciscan writer was able to lay claim to that primacy within the Catholic world on the basis of the blood tribute shed by the order of Saint Francis: among the 26 martyrs of Nagasaki, 17 were Japanese faithful, just 3 Jesuits, and as many as 6 Franciscans – who were, however, the very cause of the massacre due to their brazen and provocative attitude. In those pages, the position of the Jesuits appears wholly subordinated to the emphasis placed on the Franciscan martyrs. It is therefore not surprising that the Society, wounded in its pride and attacked for the missionary strategies adopted in a land considered for decades to be its exclusive domain, felt the need to react and reply to the offensive of their rivals in writing as well, at the level of propaganda.

Right from the first pages, Fróis claims the centrality and success of the Jesuits' work in the evangelization of the Japanese archipelago and does not fail to laud the strategy adopted from 1587 onwards – that is, after the first anti-Christian ban. Namely, on the basis of Valignano's indications, the Jesuits, Fróis acknowledges, had since then embraced a more cautious and dissembling strategy and *modus operandi*, precisely to allow the faith to flourish despite Hideyoshi's prohibitions. The new line, identified in the previous pages as the symbolism of the cross hidden in the tree, had borne fruit and allowed the Jesuits to considerably extend their influence, not only through the multiplication of conversions among the peasants of the countryside, but above all at the top of Japanese society. The *accomodatio* advocated by Valignano had, in fact, allowed the fathers to integrate even better within the Japanese aristocracy, no longer disturbed by the way of dressing and behaving of those barbarian priests who came from the sea. The extraordinary experiment of cultural openness that the Jesuits had demonstrated ended up further strengthening the Christian presence in the Far East, but nevertheless aroused a negative reaction from the Roman authorities.[15]

One cannot therefore fail to read in the words of Fróis an indirect criticism of the brazen and imprudent attitude adopted by the Franciscans. Fróis was intent on justifying the caution and feigning of his confreres. For the Portuguese priest, martyrdom pursued through blood, evoked so many times by the Jesuit writings themselves and exalted by the Franciscans, basically required less courage and less commitment than a daily martyrdom made up of a thousand precautions, infinite anguish and incalculable humiliation. An ongoing martyrdom without bloodshed, but no less heroic and certainly more useful for the propagation of the Christian faith in those lands, which by then had become hostile.[16] And in recounting the weeks that preceded the 26 crucifixions in Nagasaki, Fróis does not fail to praise the prudence with which the local leaders of the Society, in particular Father Organtino, directed his confreres, inviting them to flee, to reach safety and to hide the evidence of their work and of their very presence, so as not to endanger the numerous Christians hidden throughout south-central Japan.[17] The great proclamations regarding the "joy" with which the fathers declared their willingness to face martyrdom in their letters sent to Europe corresponded to the concrete reality of the mission, with behavior aimed at saving what could be saved, so as not to allow the destruction of that "Church, planted with so many struggles, and maintained with as many difficulties" for decades. Fróis's text, therefore, depicts Jesuits in disguise, who climb down from windows to escape the governor of Miyako's guards, but it also depicts missionaries who try everything in order to save their arrested brothers, turning to the most influential friends at court or even resorting to the corruption of members of the imperial circle.

To justify such attitudes that had very little to do with a spontaneous vocation to martyrdom, the Portuguese Jesuit did not hesitate to hark back to the early Church, which had also been subjected to terrible persecutions. In particular, he refers to Saint Paul, the evangelizing apostle whose example and doctrine were imbued in the Jesuit mentality. After having fled the capital for the first time, Fathers Organtino and Rodriguez let themselves be convinced again by the faithful not to give themselves up to their enemies, but to flee to Osaka, "in this imitating Saint Paul, who in a similar incident allowed himself to be dropped down from the walls of Damascus."[18] The reference is not a simple display of scriptural knowledge, but rather a conscious desire to reconnect with the most authentic identity of the Jesuits, who were inspired by the Nicodemitic prudence of Paul from their earliest years. But just like Paul, despite not having stubbornly sought it, they wound up not rejecting martyrdom, but rather accepting it as a gift and sign of divine election. Indeed, three members of the Society were among the 26 martyrs of Nagasaki.

In the final pages of his little book, Fróis does not forget to close the circle, explicitly recalling the prophecies of the crosses that appeared in the trees in 1589 and 1592, which can finally be correctly interpreted in the light of the crosses of martyrdom. However, it is worth emphasizing that, significantly, the Jesuit does not mention the alleged miracle of the crosses of fire that appeared on the martyrs' crosses, which instead recurs in the Franciscan reports. In line with the direction chosen in those same years by the bishop of Nagasaki, Luís Cerqueira, also a Jesuit,[19] the objective was in fact to weaken both the supernatural miraculous dimension and the exceptional nature of the Nagasaki martyrdom, overly associated with the Franciscans, and to include those events as part of the continuity of the Jesuit presence in Japan. Some testimonies taken from the beatification process of the martyrs of Nagasaki also led in the same direction: in the months following the dramatic episode, some Christian converts planted sacred trees in the place where the crosses of passion had arisen, which were soon venerated by the faithful,[20] confirming a uninterrupted circularity between different cult objects perceived as superimposable. Thus, the whole experience and hidden-most meaning of Japanese Christianity is consummated around the Christian symbol par excellence: the cross – planted in the fields, inscribed on the trunks of trees, and finally embraced by the martyrs, soaking it with their blood.

The Catholicism of the Counter-Reformation was able to turn the tragic experience in Nagasaki into a symbol and an object of propaganda on a global level, as demonstrated by the hundreds of publications dedicated to the martyrs not only in Europe, but also in the South American colonies controlled by the Spanish for at least the entire seventeenth century. These were reports and accounts written by eyewitnesses, as well as chronicles, theatrical works, poems or even homilies, in which writers and preachers who had never set foot in Japan exalted the deeds of the martyrs, recounted their heroism, with the common aim of making them usable models not only for the faithful in European Catholic dioceses, but also of the rest of the world, in particular for the Philippines and the territories of what was known as New Spain.[21] Talking about the Japanese martyrs became a way to give value – on a political, economic and religious level – to the Spanish crown's possessions in the Pacific Ocean, recently occupied lands, such as the Philippines, or even the Central and South American colonies, which became operational platforms for the missionaries destined for the Japanese archipelago.[22]

But the reasons for that interest in the theme of martyrdom also depended on something else: the desire to educate the Catholic faithful of the rest of the world by proposing heroic examples of dedication to the faith, as well as the desire to attract new missionaries and obtain funds from generous patrons for the mission. By spreading their own account of those tragic events throughout the world, the religious orders competing with each other in the task of evangelizing the Japanese archipelago also intended to reiterate their own cause, exalting the work of their own members to the detriment of those of the rival orders. This process was highly dependent on the ability to publish in several cities and to have translations into other languages, in addition to Spanish and Italian, which were dominant for obvious political and religious reasons. The Jesuits demonstrated better than the others that they could count on a truly global network, enabling them to publish more and disseminate more effectively, from Rome to the rest of Europe, making use of a formidable team of translators and printers.[23] Dominicans and Franciscans, on the contrary, published mostly within the Spanish world, above all in Madrid, but with a specific extra-European anchorage – respectively Mexico City for the

Franciscans and Manila for the Dominicans, who made use of various local printers, as well as Chinese and Japanese ones.[24]

Ultimately the theme of bloody martyrdom, initially fueled and exploited by the Franciscans and Dominicans precisely to put the more numerous Jesuits in difficulty, nearly ended up becoming the prerogative of the latter, who were able to assert their superior know-how, their global networks of colleges, their habit of writing and storytelling, as well as the ability to translate texts into various languages, from Latin to German, from French to English to Polish, and publish them almost simultaneously in multiple cities on different continents. Their extraordinary flexibility emerged once again in adapting to new situations, elaborating complex answers to unexpected problems, and in appropriating their rivals' arguments. When they lost their mission's extended presence on Japanese soil after the expulsion of the priests in 1614, they did not hesitate to embrace the thesis, initially Franciscan, of Japan as a land of martyrs and persecutors. For the Jesuits, as had been the case for the discalced Franciscans, Japan – which by then was in the process of de-Christianization – became the mirror through which to structure and relaunch their own missionary identity. On a local basis, the Catholicism under construction in the Philippines and in Central and South America owed much to the example of the martyred missionaries in Japan, who contributed to consolidating the local religious identity. This was demonstrated above all by the case of the Franciscan martyr Felipe de Jesús (de las Casas), who died in Nagasaki in 1597 and was promptly elevated to patron of his hometown, Mexico City.[25]

## The Japanese roses of Nagasaki

The Society of Jesus – and before them the Franciscan order – built the myth of a missionary holiness culminating in the ultimate sacrifice on those bloody crosses and on the martyrdom of Japanese missionaries and converts. Thus Japan became for all intents and purposes a land of persecution and holy martyrs. Thirty years after those tragic events, in the summer of 1627, Pope Urban VIII beatified the 26 Christian martyrs who died in the Japan of the bonzes and samurai. What moved the pontiff toward that far-from-obvious step in years of drastic tightening of the procedures for sanctification of candidates were, in addition to the fame of their death *in odium fidei* at the hands of bloodthirsty Japanese warriors, the "many miracles, with the approved processes" that had followed, so that thereafter, in honor of those "holy martyrs," it would have been lawful to "celebrate mass."[26] In spite of the words collected in the documentation now conserved in the Archives of the Society of Jesus, those 26 had to wait over two centuries to achieve sanctity, until well into the nineteenth century, confirming the obstacles posed by the Counter-Reformation Church to prevent the flourishing of overly spontaneous, uncontrolled cults.[27]

*The wood of martyrdom* 71

Despite the prohibitions, decrees and attempts to nip in the bud the paths to the altars of aspiring saints, for those 26, still only blessed, in Rome

> on the evening of that day and the following evening there was great joy for the Zoccolanti friars at the Church of Araceli, with great quantity of fires and lights and fireworks, and sounds of trumpets, and drums and bells and the boom of bomblets exposing the spectacle of martyrdom in a large and beautifully painted picture with their names and trials and other such notable things.[28]

Similarly, a few months later, also in Rome, on February 5, 1628, the date of the anniversary of the martyrdom of Nagasaki, the other order involved in that beatification, the Society of Jesus, spared no expense in celebrating its three beatified martyrs the previous year. Despite the fact that from the beginning of the century the popes had reiterated the ban on honoring in an overly ostentatious manner men and women who had not yet ascended to the honors of the altars,[29] and precisely in line with Ignatius of Loyola's cult of images, the Jesuits decorated the Church of Jesus and placed a large picture with the three martyrs of their Society "in whose honor the Mass and solemn office was said with music and various instruments," followed by a feast with illuminated "lanterns," "trumpets and drums and mortars exploding all around."[30]

In the same years, after decades of struggles within the Church, the hard line on the control of sanctity asserted itself, advocated by the Inquisition and by the more conservative part of the curia, which was opposed to the multiplication of spontaneous cults rising up from below, and above all determined to impose a rigorous centralization to the sanctification process, in competition with the ancient custom of local bishops governing the saint-making process. In that battle, wholly internal to the Counter-Reformation, the Jesuits placed themselves on the opposite front, alongside the diocesan leaders and Filippo Neri's Oratorians, convinced that it was necessary to reach a satisfactory compromise between the desire for papal centralization and control, on the one hand, and the maintenance of a certain local autonomy and flexibility, on the other, so as to guarantee the spontaneous development of new cults, coming also from the periphery of Catholicism, from those distant continents which had recently seen the fruits of faith flourish thanks to the generous work of missionaries.[31]

The Pope Urban VIII's decrees from 1625 to 1634 led to the victory of the intransigent line and for centuries conditioned the possibility of easy access to sainthood for numerous candidates and martyrs. Yet different interpretations of holiness did not cease to circulate in the Catholic world, giving life to a sort of polycentrism and horizontality in which Rome's authority imposed a certain attitude at a central level, without being able to eradicate different propensities in the body of the Church. As has been pointed out, the saints and beatified of the Counter-Reformation were, in large part, expressions of a Church triumphant and obedient to the hierarchies. Among the few canonized were those in line with inquisitorial and Rome-centric dictates: founders of new or reformers of old religious orders; men engaged in charitable activities; exemplary bishops such as Carlo Borromeo, notwithstanding his autonomy with respect to the curia; as well as mystics, such as Teresa of Avila, and missionaries, such as Francis Xavier, who were protagonists of the Catholic faith's global diffusion. There was less space for different, albeit equally significant figures of that season of Catholicism, figures often overlapping with missionaries, such as the martyrs who died among infidels and heretics.[32]

With the beginning of the persecutions, the land of the samurai became the land of martyrs for the faithful of Old Europe, a land of heinous persecutions, of ruthless tyrants who, following the model of the ancient pagan emperors, did not hesitate to unleash their wrath and ferociously shed the blood of Christians. But in this way Roman Catholicism was able to match the many Protestant martyrs with their own heroes – Catholics who died to defend the pope's doctrine in remote lands. In the collective imagination, Japan established itself as a land of martyrs, especially since by now, following its closure toward Westerners imposed by the new Tokugawa regime, any desire to expand the missionary presence and convert the Japanese archipelago had vanished. During the seventeenth century, although not yet canonized and despite the prohibitions of the Inquisition, the Japanese martyrs were represented on the walls of churches and Jesuit colleges, and their stories were recounted in various histories of the order, martyrologies and above all letters sent from the Far East.[33] As can be seen from the study of the *Indipetae* from the mid-seventeenth century, for the young novices eager to go on a mission for the sake of Christ and the Gospel, the Japanese archipelago thus became a land of choice, capable of ensuring martyrdom.[34]

Various testimonies exist regarding the European reception of those martyrs from the distant Indies, including the homilies of the well-known Theatine preacher and bishop of Tortona, Paolo Aresi, who in the course of 1628 dedicated some of his homilies to the blessed Japanese martyrs.[35] Aresi had learned of the vicissitudes of those heroes of the East Indies – "characters highly honored in the century, and adorned with the chivalrous dress of Spain," transformed into "celestial knights, and knights of the grand cross" – not only by reading their stories, the numerous letters sent by the Asiatic mission, but also by the voice of witnesses such as a "very ancient father" of the Franciscan order.[36] His words are useful for understanding the transmission in Italy of the early seventeenth century of the limited experience of missionaries on the other side of the globe – months, if not years, of navigation from the European coasts – in the daily pastoral practice of a parish in mid-Counter-Reformation North Italy. Through the mediation of the bishop preacher we can observe the transformation of those heroic events, though they may be light years away from the faith Italian Catholics experienced, into models of inspiration for the lives of older Christians, who paradoxically had a lot to learn from the new converts of the Far East.[37]

Paolo Aresi's account of the Nagasaki martyrdom insists above all on the full correspondence between the death on the cross of those men and that of Christ, as "living images, or life-like portraits of our Lord crucified," in a perspective of maximum identification typical of Ignatian religiosity.[38] But then, according to a characteristic model of seventeenth-century Italian preachers, the Theatine tends to transform the content of his words into metaphorical images, better if exotic and capable of arousing amazement and wonder, and above all more easily memorable, with the aim of striking the imagination of the faithful listening.[39] In the barren field of idolatrous Japan these "sacred roses" had arisen, "the first fruits of the Japanese field, the first flowers of that new Church, the early fruits of that great field that has grown wild and sterile up to this hour." Models for the universal Church, those martyrs were above all the vanguard of the spread of Christianity in pagan and idolatrous lands, capable with their sacrifice of triggering a virtuous mechanism converting peoples who had to that point remained foreign to the faith of the Gospel. Tertullian's well-known adage that "the blood of martyrs is the seed of the Church" was thus taken up and adapted in various forms, combining it with other pervasive images. Those men were compared not only to roses in the desert of idolatry, but also to palm trees, playing on the concept of martyrdom obtained as a reward for their faith. They also alluded to the desert tree able to offer a perspective on the journey to the heavenly city. Perhaps inspired by the Jesuit missionary Luís Fróis, always attentive to grasping the naturalistic as well as the ethnographic particularities of the archipelago,[40] one palm especially attracted the bishop-preacher's attention, "proper to the Japanese island, which is of such a strange nature, it putrefies when wet, and then dies, but when cut and exposed to the sun, it regains life and turns green again."[41]

Through parallels with classical mythology, characteristic of early seventeenth-century oratory,[42] Aresi emphasized the exceptional nature of the martyrs' combat, drawing strength from their contact with the cross, of which, as Christians, they were children, unlike the Japanese enemies, "unaccustomed to fighting on the cross" because they are "enemies of the cross."[43] "These blessed fathers of ours, on the contrary, led their entire lives among the crosses, the cross continuously embraced and carried, spurning luxury and delectable tables."[44] In the process of unification and full identification with the passion of Christ, those martyrs went beyond – the bishop affirmed in a surge of enthusiasm at the limit of orthodoxy – because they had been pierced with spears not while dead, like the Nazarene, but while alive.

As exemplary cases of Christians ready to die for their faith, the Japanese martyrs also represented a model for the European faithful. Although there were "through the mercy of the Lord no persecutors of the faith in the diocese of Tortona, against whom we have to fight," nevertheless, the bishop warned, "we do not lack other domestic enemies, our disorderly passions, our unbridled appetites, this our restless and rebellious flesh, these badly accustomed senses of ours […]." The transposition of missionary heroism into the everyday life of the lands here below ended with an appeal that attempted to keep together the dazzling image of the missionary martyrs with the need for a renewal of the religious and spiritual life of Old Europe at the time of the Counter-Reformation

> Oh Christian, one does not seek from you that you shed blood, that you expose your chest to lances, that you stretch your arms and the body upon the Cross, but it is good that you forgive the wrongs, that you love that enemy of yours, that you restrain your sensual appetite, that you observe the commandments of God, and in this way, you too shall be victorious and enjoy the Society of Martyrs.[45]

In this way those events – geographically as well as culturally distant from Old Europe – acquired meaning. They became models for a moral, devout and fully Christian life. Just as in the past the martyrs of the primitive Church functioned as ideal guides for the Christians of the following centuries. Now those converts from the Far East, contemporary in time but very distant in space, became analogous sources of inspiration. If the century of saints had passed in the West, things went differently on the other side of the planet, in those recently discovered districts, where they could once again be seen "still in our times":

> Courageous martyrs, glorious saints, heroic men; if we are not such, there is no excuse, the fault is all ours […] Behold how from the East Indies, from countries unknown for many thousands of years, from the New World, saints arise, who enjoy Heaven […] We, like ancient Christians, should be mirrors and examples of holiness to the new church of India; but since we are not such, let us at least be ashamed of not following their glorious footsteps, and not imitating their examples.[46]

The sermon concluded thus with a surprising reversal of the hierarchies between Europe, which had been Christian for centuries, and the lands of the new mission, held up as guides for a European Christianity now tired and unable to regain momentum in the name of faith after the internal divisions of the sixteenth century. Attesting to the widespread interpretation of the Nagasaki martyrs' experience as pedagogical models for the faithful of the Po Valley, for example, is a canvas commissioned for the chapels of the sanctuary of the Sacro Monte di Varallo and painted by the artist Tanzio da Varallo, now kept in Milan's Pinacoteca di Brera, which depicted the massacre of the

23 Franciscan martyrs – confirming the persistence of a divided and divisive memory of the episode.[47]

But the story of the beatified Japanese was also an opportunity for the Catholic hierarchs to clearly reiterate a specific interpretation of martyrdom: those Japanese missionaries and Christians could be considered true martyrs because their blood had been shed and they were killed by their executioners; they had died *in odium fidei*. All the others, who had equally suffered persecution in the name of faith, despite their commendable conduct and fidelity shown to the Gospel at the price of exile and the loss of all earthly goods, were not considered as such. Only the dramatic test of blood and violent death at the hands of enemies of the Christian faith allowed them to merit the palm of martyrdom. In another sermon dedicated to the 23 blessed Franciscans, the bishop of Tortona was in fact keen to clarify the distance that separated one from the other, establishing a sort of hierarchy of suffering among the victims of persecution in the name of faith:

> The loss of things, reputation, relatives, children, are crosses, and very serious tribulations, fasting, disciplines, cloistered mortifications are certainly heavy crosses, it is true, but they have nothing to do with the shedding of one's blood and loss of life.[48]

However, in the same years, alongside a more rigorous and clear-cut interpretation, of which the Theatine bishop became the spokesman, other ways of understanding martyrdom survived that were not systematically associated with violent death. A broader meaning, for example, was proposed by the Jesuit Théophile Raynaud, who in the first part of the seventeenth century considered worthy of the palm of martyrdom those priests who had dedicated themselves to alleviating the suffering of others during a plague outbreak and who had lost their lives as a result. In essence, a "martyrdom of charity" lived through a "daily cross," made up of obedience, perseverance, sacrifice and suffering spread over time. In turn, even the Barnabites and Camillians adhered to this broader meaning of the term martyrdom, connected with assistance to the sick. Nevertheless, they encountered the censure and hostility of the Roman Inquisition, the Dominicans and influential circles of the curia.[49]

In the context of the Japanese mission, as we have seen – initially on the initiative of the Franciscans followed only later by the Jesuits – the Nagasaki massacre episode led to a turning point which gradually identified that missionary land with the heroic and bloody model of the martyrs tortured and killed on the cross by the fierce samurai of the shogun. At the same time a negative conception of the Japanese and their land was fixed in the imagination of European readers and faithful. From the outset, as pointed out by Guido Mongini, the Jesuit identity was rooted in a culture of martyrdom, which had been at the basis of Ignatius of Loyola's experience, and which then remained an essential feature of the way of thinking about the faith from part of the members of the Society.[50] The study of the *Indipetae* clearly demonstrated that the ambition to shed blood for the faith became a recurring motif in the vocations of young aspiring missionaries, who sought full identification with Christ through the sacrifice of their lives.[51] In this process the example of the English martyrs during the 1580s played a decisive role,[52] followed by the Japanese example, about which the numerous annual letters from the East, promptly printed and translated into various European languages, provided details to the European public.[53]

And yet – confirming the fluidity of definitions, and in spite of the attempts to fix and catalog the aspiring saints[54] – in that same missionary laboratory that was the Far East, martyrdom was also understood in a less restrictive sense, a meaning that remained in the minority but did not completely disappear. There was an alternative model, which better corresponded to the project of missionary expansion through the strategy of accommodation in the Land of the Rising Sun. It came in the decades preceding the persecutions, when the spread of Christianity still seemed as if it could be accomplished peacefully and with the approval of the local political authorities. In the writings of the Society, that second model of the path to martyrdom and holiness was identified with one figure in particular: the Christian daimyo Takayama Ukon, known as Justo.

## Notes

1. Refer to the compelling book by Gian Carlo Roscioni, *Il desiderio delle Indie. Storie, sogni e fughe di giovani gesuiti italiani*, Torino, Einaudi, 2001; see also Adriano Prosperi, *La vocazione. Storie di gesuiti tra Cinquecento e Seicento*, Torino, Einaudi, 2016, pp. 75–97.
2. Imbruglia, *La milizia come «maniera di vivere» dei gesuiti: missione, martirio obbedienza*, cit.; on the construction of the concept of martyrdom in the first centuries of the early Church cf. Glen W. Bowersock, *Martyrdom and Rome*, Cambridge, Cambridge University Press, 1995.
3. Pizzorusso, *Il martirio* in odium fidei *dalla realtà missionaria alla burocrazia romana*, cit., pp. 183–84.
4. It should be noted, however, that the vocation to martyrdom was a topic of discussion within the Jesuit order, and aroused a certain distrust in the first decades: the difficulty for the leaders of the order was to find a middle ground between a legitimate, and indeed encouraged, tension towards self-sacrifice in the name of God, and an over-sought martyrdom, which imprudently risked revealing a presumptuous desire for personal affirmation (Guido Mongini, *L'apostolo gesuitico tra propaganda religiosa e autoconservazione. Aspetti del martirio nella Compagnia di Gesù (1540–1580)*, in «Annali di scienze religiose», 12 (2019), pp. 11–49).
5. Among the numerous works on the martyrs of Nagasaki cf. at least Hesselink, *The Dream of Christian Nagasaki*, cit., pp. 108–16; Hélène Vu Thanh, *The Glorious Martyrdom of the Cross. The Franciscans and the Japanese Persecutions of 1597*, in «Culture & History Digital Journal», 6/1, (2017), http://dx.doi.org/10.3989/chdj.2017.005; Tronu Montane, *Sacred Space and Ritual in Early Modern Japan*, cit., pp. 131–35.

The wood of martyrdom 77

6 In the account of his journey around the world, Carletti dwells at length on the episode, detailing the macabre details of the torture of Christian martyrs (Francesco Carletti, *Ragionamenti del mio viaggio intorno al mondo*, Milano, Mursia, 2015, pp. 99–106).
7 Luis Fróis, *Relatione della gloriosa morte di XXVI posti in croce per comandamento del re di Giappone, alli 5 di febraio 1597...*, Milano, Pacifico Pontio, 1599, pp. 8–12.
8 Juan de Santa María, *Relatione del martirio che sei padri scalzi di San Francesco et venti giaponesi christiani patirono nel Giapone l'anno 1597*, Roma, Niccolò Muzi, 1599. Cfr. Roldán-Figueroa, *The Martyrs of Japan*, cit., pp. 104–5.
9 As early as 1583, the Visitor of the Indies, Alessandro Valignano, had warned the Roman authorities of the danger represented by a possible landing in Japan of other religious orders, foreseeing the negative reactions from the Japanese (Valignano, *Sumario de las cosas de Japon (1583)*, cit., pp. 143–49). On the barefoot Franciscans, also known as "alcantarini," a new Franciscan family that arose in Spain at the beginning of the sixteenth century, cf. cfr. Roldán-Figueroa, *The Martyrs of Japan*, cit., pp. 220–46.
10 Imbruglia, *The Jesuit Missions of Paraguay and a Cultural History of Utopia (1568–1789)*, cit., pp. 3–21.
11 Bartoli, *Dell'Historia della Compagnia*, pp. 104–5; Vu Thanh, *The Glorious Martyrdom of the Cross*, cit., pp. 6–8.
12 Juan de Santa María, *Relatione del martirio*, cit., pp. 79–93.
13 Ivi, pp. 26–29, 39–40, 102. On the criticism of the work of the Jesuits in Japan by the Franciscans cf. also Lage Reis Correia, *Violence, Identity and Conscience in the Context of the Japanese Catholic Missions (16th Century)*, cit., pp. 115–16.
14 Hideyoshi would have welcomed the Franciscans who landed in Japan with these words: "These are true Christians" (Juan de Santa María, *Relatione del martirio*, cit., p. 29).
15 In response to the sending of the *Cerimoniale*, on 24 December 1585 Acquaviva openly contested the strategy adopted by Valignano, precisely insisting on the need not to hide the "virtue of the cross": "Whoever preaches this doctrine, I don't know why he should of the Cross and the imitation of Christ who preaches for God, who advised and showed by example voluntary poverty and contempt for everything worldly." (Valignano, *Il cerimoniale per i missionari del Giappone*, cit., pp. 320–21).
16 Fróis, *Relatione della gloriosa morte*, cit., p. 7.
17 Ivi, pp. 26, 30, 43.
18 "in questo imitando san Paolo, che in simile accidente si lasciò da fratelli calar in una sporta giù dalle mura di Damasco" (Ivi, p. 29).
19 Vu Thanh, *The Glorious Martyrdom of the Cross*, cit., pp. 6–7.
20 Omata Rappo, *Des indes lointaines aux scènes des collèges*, cit., p. 156.
21 Roldán-Figueroa, *The Martyrs of Japan*, cit.
22 Ivi, pp. 36–38.
23 Ivi, pp. 115–21; Romano, *Impressions de Chine*, cit., pp. pp. 38–43.
24 Roldán-Figueroa, *The Martyrs of Japan*, cit., pp. 121–42.
25 Ivi, pp. 247–56.
26 Archivum Historicum Societatis Iesu Romanum (ARSI), Postul. Gen. (santi e beati), Martiri giapponesi, busta 851, doc. 1.
27 Omata Rappo, *Des Indes lointaines aux scènes des collèges*, cit., pp. 131–83.
28 "la sera di quel giorno et la sera seguente si fece grandissima allegrezza nella Chiesa dell'Araceli dalli frati Zoccolanti con gran quantità di fuochi e luminarii e fochi artificiali, e suoni di trombe, e tamburi e campane e romori di mortaletti con esponere in un quadro grande e di bellissima pittura lo spettacolo del martirio con

i nomi et processo di essi e altre cose sì ragguardevoli" (ARSI, Postul. Gen. (santi e beati), Martiri giapponesi, busta 851, doc. 1).

29 Simon Ditchfield, *Il mondo della Riforma e della Controriforma*, in *Storia della santità nel cristianesimo occidentale*, Roma, Viella, 2005, p. 285.

30 "in honor de quali fu detta la Messa et l'officio solenne con musiche et diversi istrumenti […] lanternoni illuminati […] trombe e tamburi e mortaletti che furono intorno sparati" (ARSI, Postul. Gen. (santi e beati), Martiri giapponesi, busta 851, doc. 1). The same document with minimal transcription inaccuracies is cited in Omata Rappo, *Des Indes lointaines aux scènes des collèges*, cit., p. 164. On the Roman feasts on the occasion of canonizations cf. Silvia Carandini, *L'effimero spirituale. Feste e manifestazioni religiose nella Roma dei papi in età moderna*, in *Storia d'Italia. Annali, 16: Roma, la città del papa: vita civile e religiosa dal giubileo di Bonifacio 8. al giubileo di papa Wojtyla*, ed. Luigi Fiorani e Adriano Prosperi, Torino, Einaudi, 2000, pp. 521–53; Fernando Quiles García, José Jaime García Bernal, Paolo Broggio, Marcello Fagiolo Dell'Arco (ed.), *A la luz de Roma. Santos y santidad en el barroco iberoamericano*, Roma-Sevilla, Roma Tre Press-Enredars/Universidad Pablo de Olavide, 2020; Vittorio Casale, *Gloria ai beati e ai santi: le feste di beatificazione e di canonizzazione*, in Marcello Fagiolo (ed.), *La festa a Roma dal Rinascimento al 1870*, Torino, Umberto Allemandi & C., 1997, pp. 124–41.

31 Miguel Gotor, *I beati del papa. Santità, Inquisizione e obbedienza in età moderna*, Firenze, Olschki, 2002, pp. 138–48.

32 Ronnie Po-chia Hsia, *La Controriforma*. cit. pp. 169–75; Miguel Gotor, *Chiesa e santità nell'Italia moderna*, Roma-Bari, Laterza, 2004, pp. 93–103; Ditchfield, *Il mondo della Riforma e della Controriforma*, cit., pp. 293–97; Pizzorusso, *Il martirio* in odium fidei *dalla realtà missionaria alla burocrazia romana*, cit., pp. 196–97.

33 See, for example, the exhibition on the occasion of the canonization of Ignatius and Francis Xavier in 1622 inside the Church of Gesù of the images of 120 martyrs, including the three Jesuits of Nagasaki (Emanuele Colombo, *Lacrime e sangue. Martirio e missione nella Compagnia di Gesù in età moderna*, in «Annali di scienze religiose», XII (2019), p. 65). On the production of images of martyrs and their dissemination by the Jesuits cf. Ditchfield, *Il mondo della Riforma e della Controriforma*, cit., pp. 273–75.

34 Colombo, *Lacrime e sangue*, cit., pp. 85–89, 94–104.

35 Francisco Andreu, *Arese, Paolo*, in *Dizionario biografico degli italiani*, 4 (1962), pp. 84–85; see also Erminia Ardissino, *Il barocco e il sacro: la predicazione del teatino Paolo Aresi tra letteratura, immagini e scienza*, Città del Vaticano, Libreria Editrice Vaticana, 2001, pp. 151–56.

36 "personaggi honoratissimi al secolo, e ornati deli habito cavalleresco di Spagna […] cavalieri celesti, e cavalieri della gran croce"; "padre molto antico" (Paolo Aresi, *De Cavalieri della Gran Croce, sermone di monsignor Paolo Aresi vescovo di Tortona. Fatto in lode di ventitré martiri del Giappone, seguaci del serafico Padre San Francesco, fra min. osservanti. Nella chiesa di S.Maria delle Gratie in Voghera, con occasione della festa, che si celebrò degli istessi Beati, il giorno 17 di settembre del 1628*, Tortona, per Pietro Giovanni Calenzano et Eliseo Viola compagni, 1628, p. 20).

37 The approach of the Jesuit Luis de Guzmán in his *Historia de las missiones* is no different; see Roldán-Figueroa, *The Martyrs of Japan*, cit., pp. 164–72.

38 P. Aresi, *Le rose giapponesi, sermone di monsignor Paolo Aresi vescovo di Tortona. Della bellezza di tre martiri del Giappone religiosi della Compagnia di Giesù. Fatto in Castelnovo nell'occasione della festa, che ivi si celebrò degli istessi Beati martiri li 6 febraro 1628*, Tortona, per Pier Giovanni Calenzano, et Eliseo Viola compagni, 1628, p. 14.

39 Erminia Ardissino, *Caratteri della predicazione in età federiciana*. *Gli scritti di Paolo Aresi e le prediche in duomo per san Carlo*, in «Studia Borromaica», 21 (2007), pp. 283–86.
40 In his well-known treatise on the differences between Europeans and Japanese, the palm does not appear among the plants mentioned, just as he does not seem to mention it in his other writings (Fróis, *Européens et Japonais*, cit., pp. 75–76; Castel-Branco, Carvalho, *Luis Frois: First Western Accounts of Japan's Gardens, Cities and Landscapes*, cit.).
41 "propria dell'isola giapponese, la quale è di natura tanto strana, che bagnata putrefassi, e muore, tagliata, et esposta al sole riacquista la vita, e rinverdisce" (Paolo Aresi, *Le Palme giapponesi, sermone di monsignor Paolo Aresi vescovo di Tortona. Delle vittorie di ventitré martiri del Giappone, seguaci del serafico Padre S. Francesco fra min. osservanti. Fatto da lui nella chiesa della Pace in Castelnuovo, con occasione della Festa, che si celebrò degli istessi Beati li 5 febbraro 1628*, In Tortona, per Pietro Giovanni Calenzano, et Eliseo Viola compagni, 1628, pp. 9–10).
42 Ardissino, *Caratteri della predicazione in età federiciana*, cit., p. 286.
43 The comparison was with the giant Antaeus, who in the fight against Hercules had drawn his strength from contact with mother Earth. On the use of examples drawn from other sciences in Aresi's homiletics and for his encyclopaedic vocation cf. Ardissino, *Il barocco e il sacro*, cit., pp. 244–50.
44 "Questi nostri beati padri all'opposto tutta la vita loro menata havevano fra le croci, la croce continuamente abbracciata, e portata, e niente prattichi delle laute, e delicate mense" (Aresi, *Le Palme giapponesi*, cit., p. 11).
45 "Non si cerca da te, o Christiano, che versi il sangue, che lanciate esponga il petto, che distenda le braccia, et il corpo in Croce, ma si bene che perdoni l'ingiurie, che ami quel tuo inimico, che raffreni quel tuo sensuale appettito, che osservi i comandamenti di Dio, che in questa guisa, anche tu sarai vincitore, e goderai la Compagnia de Martiri" (*Ivi*, p. 18).
46 "De coraggiosi martiri, de santi gloriosi, degli homini heroici; e però se noi tali non siamo, non v'è scusa, la colpa è tutta nostra […] Ecco che dall'Indie orientali, da paesi tante migliaie di anni non conosciuti, dal Mondo nuovo sorgono de Santi, che vanno a godere il Paradiso […] Doveremmo noi come Christiani antichi essere specchio et esemplari di santità alla novella chiesa dell'India, ma poiché tali non siamo, vergogniamoci almeno di non seguire le loro gloriose pedate, e non imitare il loro esempi" (*Ibidem*).
47 Tanzio da Varallo, *Il martirio dei Beati francescani a Nagasaki*, circa 1627, oil on canvas, 115x80 cm https://pinacotecabrera.org/collezione-online/opere/il-martirio-dei-santi-francescani-a-nagasaki/.
48 "Il perder la robba, la riputatione, i parenti, i figli, sono croci, e tribolationi assai gravi, i digiuni, le discipline, le mortificationi claustrali sono croci non poco pesanti, egli è vero, ma non hanno tuttavia che fare con lo spargimento del proprio sangue, e la perdita della vita" (Aresi, *De Cavalieri della Gran Croce*, cit., p. 8).
49 Jean-Pascal Gay, *Finding Martyrs at Home?: Jesuit Attempts at Redefining Martyrdom in the Seventeenth Century and Their Censure*, in «Journal of Jesuit Studies», 9 (2022), pp. 15–35.
50 Mongini, *Maschere dell'identità*, cit., pp. 22–31, 420–29; Colombo, *Lacrime e sangue*, cit., pp. 65–68.
51 *Cinque secoli di Litterae indipetae. Il desiderio delle missioni nella Compagnia di Gesù*, a cura di Girolamo. Imbruglia, Pierre-Antoine Fabre, Guido Mongini, Roma, Institutum Historicum Societatis Iesu, 2022.
52 Eleonora Rai, *Spargere il sangue per Cristo. La vocazione al martirio missionario come elemento di identità gesuitica: il caso di John Ogilvie (1579–1615)*, in

«Rivista storica italiana», CXXXII 3 (2020), pp. 1028–30. For the lack of references to the theme of martyrdom in the first Indipetae cf. Mongini, *L'apostolo gesuitico tra propaganda religiosa e autoconservazione*, cit., pp. 14–21.

53 Fabre, *La question missionnaire dans la Compagnie de Jésus*, cit., pp. 344–45.
54 The canonical distinction between a "martyr," who died *in odium fidei*, and a "confessor of the faith," to mean those who have suffered exile and persecution but without the sacrifice of their lives, appears more as a later attempt to bring order than an effective instrument of understanding of the history of holiness in the modern age (Pizzorusso, *Il martirio* in odium fidei *dalla realtà missionaria alla burocrazia romana*, cit., pp. 187–88).

# 5 The Pope's samurai
## Takayama Ukon

### A living saint

The case of the Japanese lord Takayama Ukon undoubtedly falls among the cases of "blessed losers," since he belongs to that group of predestined to the halo who missed the goal of canonization throughout the modern age, despite the repeated attempts of his Jesuit promoters.[1] In other ways, from the point of view of a long-term history that embraces the theme of holiness from the Counter-Reformation to the prospect of building a global Church in the twenty-first century, the sixteenth-century warrior instead falls among the so-called "blessed winners": in February 2017, more than four centuries after his death, the "Pope's samurai"– as the Italian newspapers would soon dub him – crowned his long journey toward the altars with the proclamation of his beatification by Cardinal Angelo Amato in Osaka, before a square full of faithful. It is long and tortuous history, made of leaps forward, but also of numerous setbacks, a story that speaks to us of the Church of yesterday and today, of the Catholicism of the Counter-Reformation in the modern age but also of post-Vatican Council II Catholicism, interested in putting down roots in every corner of the planet, and to show its less authoritarian and clerical face. Finally, it is a complex story that speaks to us of another way of defining and thinking about holiness, which proposes a path to martyrdom without the shortcut of spectacular bloodshed.

If it is true that "saints count for how they appear, not for how they are,"[2] then to tell Takayama Ukon's story it is worth starting from the bottom, or rather from the end of his earthly trajectory, to observe how his figure was perceived by the men and women who had accompanied him on that extraordinary, and in many ways painful and dramatic journey of faith in Japan of the early modern era.

Manila, February 5, 1615. Between the solemn tolling of the bells, while the funeral procession passed through the streets and squares to accompany the coffin of the Japanese lord to the church, an increasingly insistent murmur made its way through the crowd: "the saint is dead."[3] The deceased had taken the name of Justus on the occasion of his conversion to Christianity over fifty years earlier. Members of his family and his closest circle gathered at his funeral; just a month earlier, he had left his native land with them, following the unleashing of new anti-Christian persecutions by the now unified lords. Other exponents of the increasingly large community of Japanese exiles had come to pay their last homage to the old daimyo, as did men of God, the representatives of the religious orders, in particular the Jesuits and Franciscans, as well as the king's men, the Spanish governor of the Philippines and other local authorities. Arrayed in their finest clothes, they all came to honor the one who was already revered as a saint, and who in his lifetime had been considered one of the "main pillars" of the Japanese Church. The faithful huddled together for a last farewell, rushed to embrace and kiss the feet of the "warrior of Christ," in the hope of appropriating, through physical contact, some of his charisma and saintly fragrance.

It was a recurring scene in early seventeenth-century Catholic Europe: the moment of the funeral was often the occasion to start the beatification process of a virtuous and admired man or woman, whom relatives, friends and disciples intended to raise to the honors of the altars.[4] Similarly, on the other side of the globe, in the Spanish possession of the Philippines, the last confessor of Takayama, the Jesuit missionary Pedro Morejón, took care to collect all useful information for the construction of a profile of holiness to be proposed to the confreres and later to the Roman authorities.[5] The making of the saint and the process of canonization took their first steps in the middle of the Pacific Ocean. And in the same months, in papal Viterbo, another confessor and promoter of aspirants to the halo, the Dominican friar Roberto Vittori, promoted the post-mortem cult of Francesca Vacchini da Viterbo through the distribution of images and texts in which she was depicted and defined as a saint, despite the lack of authorization from the papal authorities. Vittori was called to account for that imprudent initiative before the Holy Inquisition, determined to nip in the bud a cult that was no longer included in the catalog of models of holiness promoted by the Church of the Counter-Reformation.[6] The inquisitorial repression of devotional acts that had always been tolerated and, only from the beginning of the seventeenth century, considered unacceptable, actually concerned, at least initially, only the Italian peninsula, where the grip of the ecclesiastical institution was stronger. Thousands of kilometers away, in colonial Manila, those decrees, regulations, and Roman-centric procedures were in fact neither shared nor approved by the representatives of that same Church of the Counter-Reformation.

But who had Takayama Ukon been in the decades preceding his passing away to arouse such enthusiasm among the Christians of the Philippines? Belonging to an ancient family of daimyos originally from the central region of the Japanese archipelago, near the imperial capital, Miyako (present-day Kyoto), Ukon was the son of Takayama Zusho no Kami (Dario for the Christians), a minor feudal lord who controlled the castle of Sawa, a strategic point of access to the sea. At the time of his birth, around 1552, Japan was riven by internal struggles – the so-called "Sengoku" period – among various warlords who no longer recognized the central power of the emperor and the shogun, and who aspired to create a new order. In such a context of political and military chaos, the first Westerners made their appearance, Portuguese merchants and then Jesuit missionaries, who, following Francis Xavier, began in 1549 the ambitious attempt to spread the Christian faith in the Far East.

The conversion of Ukon and his entire clan depended instead on reasons that are partly mysterious to us today, but certainly not related to economic issues, as had been the case with the lords of Kyushu, because the Takayama lands were located far from the coasts and close to the heart of Japanese power.[7] Occurring in 1563, following a meeting with two Jesuit missionaries, Gaspar Vilela and the Japanese convert Lourenço, the spiritual conversion affected neither his samurai way of life nor the participation of father and son in the ambitious and successful attempt to unify a substantial part of the archipelago, as promoted by Oda Nobunaga.[8] Ukon superimposed his commitment to the expansion of the Catholic faith in the Land of the Rising Sun over his involvement in the political and military events of his time. Thus he became one of the main protectors of the "law of Christ," also contributing financially to support the efforts of the Jesuits with the construction, on his lands, of churches and colleges for the training of an indigenous clergy and the Christian education of young Japanese aristocrats, as Alessandro Valignano did not fail to note as early as 1583.[9]

Over the years, the adhesion to the project of missionary proselytism by important members of the Japanese ruling class such as Takayama led the Jesuit fathers to modify their strategies for Christian expansion. After an initial phase in which the Portuguese and Spanish line was imposed – convinced as they were of the need to promote the faith by any means, even by taking part in the internal struggles of Japanese society and soliciting the explicit support of the Lusitanian merchants – a perspective that was more attentive to respect for the habits, traditions and lifestyle of the local population took over. This line later took the name of "*accomodatio*," developed mainly by the Italians Alessandro Valignano and Organtino Gnecchi Soldo.[10] Aware that the absence of political and military domination by the Western crowns did not allow them the same methods of action taken in other contexts – think of Spanish America, or the part of India dominated by the Portuguese – where the expansion of trade and colonial activity had coincided with the spread of the Catholic faith, Valignano and Gnecchi promoted an adaptation of Christian faith and practices to Japanese society. High-born converts such as Takayama, who by virtue of their social status could not accept being considered exponents of inferior civilizations, destined to assimilate Western models in all respects,[11] pushed them in the same direction. On this basis, therefore, points of contact were sought between the two cultures and a common platform founded on a remarkable intellectual flexibility and full willingness to compromise on the liturgical and, in some way, even on the doctrinal level. Such an approach was not slow to arouse hostility and incomprehension within the Japanese mission itself and especially in Rome, among the leaders of the Society and within the pontifical curia, as it represented a somewhat unscrupulous and original attempt to rework the intransigent model of the Catholic Counter-Reformation.

Ukon's prestige and the respect for his military talent, his culture, and his virtuosity in the art of the tea ceremony (he was a tea master, a disciple of the famous Sen-no-Rikyū) allowed the missionaries to enter Japanese high society, and to multiply conversions within the social, political and military elite of the Japanese archipelago. Not even with the rise of Toyotomi Hideyoshi did the situation seem to change. He displayed tolerance with the missionaries and could count on the support of powerful Christian daimyos such as Ukon or Konishi Yukinaga (Agostinho).[12] Both accompanied his triumphal expedition to the south to conquer the island of Kyushu in the summer of 1587. But in the very course of the military campaign, as we have seen, Hideyoshi noted with growing concern the influence of those foreign clerics and promulgated an edict prohibiting Christianity in Japan. Unlike most, Ukon refused to bow to the diktat imposed from above. He lost everything and for several years was forced to live in exile, a semi-secrecy, on the margins of society, persecuted and in total poverty.

Only his warrior and family prestige preserved him from the inevitable martyrdom and allowed him, after a few years, to be reintegrated into the aristocratic world. However, he had to agree to move to Kanazawa, to the northern fiefdoms of the daimyo Maeda Toshiie. Far from Hideyoshi's court, Ukon and his family continued to promote, albeit with greater discretion, the spread of the Catholic faith in the region, attracting missionaries and financing the construction of sacred buildings. Around 1613–1614 the new Tokugawa regime intensified the persecutions again, and forced the Takayamas to leave Kanazawa, to cross Honshu in the middle of winter to take refuge in Nagasaki together with all the other Christians who remained in the archipelago. The shogun's peremptory order was to expel all Christian missionaries and their most influential supporters such as Ukon. In November 1614, the Takayama family embarked for Manila with the last Jesuit fathers and left the land of their ancestors forever. Following the crossing, the samurai of Christ's earthly voyage would soon come to an end, and another journey would begin – this time heavenly, but no less troubled – toward sainthood.

As in the best of Roman Catholic traditions, one did not even have to wait for Ukon's deceased body to cool down before witnessing the immediate construction of his saintly profile. Moreover, this had already appeared to his contemporaries in previous years, when his painful choice of fidelity to the Christian faith, despite the hostility of the Japanese authorities, had led him to face humiliation and harassment of all kinds under the amazed eyes of samurai and gentlewomen who, not long before, had admired and perhaps envied the qualities and power of the daimyo well integrated into the network of shogunal power. But we owe the image of Takayama as a living saint above all to the writings of the Jesuit missionaries, who did not hesitate to praise the heroic virtues of that Japanese gentleman who became a knight of Christ. And it is precisely in the letters from the East, and then in the *Historia de Japam* by one of the Jesuits, Luis Fróis, that we find the first biographical profiles of him.[13] As early as 1579, in a letter written by the missionary priest Francisco Carrión, Ukon was described as a pillar of the Christian presence in the region: "This Christianity is headed by a Christian lord called Justus, a highly esteemed person in that kingdom, and a very good Christian."[14] This was followed by the story of Ukon's betrayal of his feudal overlord, Araki Murashige, in favor of Nobunaga – what seemed to be an entirely political affair that demonstrated Ukon's flair for choosing the winning horse, but which the Jesuits interpreted in a religious key: it was above all Ukon's desire to protect the missionaries from Nobunaga's threats that led him to favor the Oda. There was also an Old Testament parallel with the story of Abraham for the choice of the Christian daimyo to sacrifice his firstborn son, left as a hostage in the hands of Araki, in order to fulfill God's will.[15]

The second decisive moment in the biography of the future blessed which recurred in Jesuit sources was the exile in the summer of 1587, following the first anti-Christian ban by Hideyoshi. In this rather disappointing panorama in the eyes of Western religious people, the figure of Ukon stood out for coherence and courage, becoming, under the pen of Luis Fróis, an almost unique example of a Japanese warrior willing to lose all temporal goods to save his soul. But according to the drafter of the annual letter, Ukon had been preparing for such a dramatic choice for years, aware that at a certain point the service of God and the shogun could come into conflict. He had thus prepared himself for persecution and eventual martyrdom ever since Nobunaga's funeral, when, in the presence of the great men of Japan, he had ostentatiously refused to take part in rites he considered idolatrous, thus exposing himself to general blame and to the "certain danger of losing his status and life."[16] He showed equal consistency toward his vassals, whom he invited to look for other lords to serve – although without ever denying their Christian faith:

> In this departure of his he did not beseech them, nor did he insistently ask them for anything other than that they be strong and constant in their Faith to the point of shedding blood and giving their lives for it; and that they live like good Christians, giving that example of virtue, which they had always given, as he hoped and trusted.[17]

In the following years, Ukon's life choices helped to make him a living legend within the Christian community of Japan, as evidenced by the description of his arrival in Nagasaki in 1589 to visit the provincial father of the Society in the archipelago. Unlike the other Christian lords, Takayama presented himself "in clothing and condition very different from the one in which we used to see him before," reported the drafter of the annual letter of 1589. In fact, he appeared "in a very positive clothing, unrecognized, as a pilgrim with only six servants, whom he also treated as companions, taking them with him covertly." And despite the privations suffered and the loss of "honor and wealth," he "was no less happy and cheerful."[18] He was presented as a latter day Job,[19] his faith put to a severe test; and the fame of his holiness had spread throughout the region, to the point that at his sight the priests were consoled and he was made the object of "extraordinary signs of love and respect" from other Christian lords, and not only.

> All the people, even women and children, greatly honored and revered him, and all sorts of people ran after him, occupying the streets where he passed in such a way that there was scarcely any room left for him to pass forward: everyone applauding around him, making a marvelous feast of his coming, they preached his virtue, praised his strength of mind, his constant piety.[20]

But what amazed the faithful most of all was Ukon's serene attitude, the "patience and joy with which he persevered in sustaining this exile with so many travails, his personal poverty and that of his home, experiencing in them a continuous desire to also shed blood and give his life for Christ."[21]

More than ten years later, in 1603, the now elderly Ukon – who had moved to the north of the island of Honshu, to Kanazawa, on the lands of the Maeda clan – recurred in the annual letters of the Portuguese Jesuit Matheo de Couros. The Jesuit emphasized his decisive role as guide of the Japanese Christian community and his activism in spreading the new faith into hitherto unreached territories, also due to the shortage of Western missionaries:

> Since in the past Justo Ukondono has always been a rare mirror of every virtue to this entire Church, so also in his devotion, and in the zeal with which he honors God, he is the principal support that those Christians have, teaching and helping everyone, never missing an opportunity to draw as many as possible to the knowledge of the true God; whence it arises, that through his zeal it increases every day, perfecting that Christianity.[22]

What is striking in the words of the Jesuit is the importance attributed to a layman, moreover Japanese, in the work of building a missionary Church in a hostile land and in a context of growing persecutions. From the following year's letter emerges his central role in converting, also through the donation of cash gifts, a bonze who had hitherto been an obstinate enemy of Christianity, as well as in convincing the provincial father to establish a new residence of the Society in Kanazawa.[23] So at that time, the old Ukon was perceived as a driving force of the missionary Christianity still alive in the Far East, and he was recognized as having an undisputed leadership role in the local community: political, economic as well as spiritual guide for the newly converted faithful.

These few testimonies, to which numerous others could be added,[24] allow us to understand how the myth of Ukon was built over the years, through the writing and circulation of missionary letters across Europe, but also in the Americas, Asia and the Philippines. And it is therefore not surprising that before his death he could be considered, even more than a martyr, a true and proper living saint.[25] Yet despite the hagiographic effort and the desire to make him an exemplary figure of an authentic Christian devoted to prayer and eager to retire to private life, the same Jesuit sources, albeit not always coherently, offer us clues about his persistent involvement in the political and military activities of his time. Even after the exile of the summer of 1587, Ukon was able to maintain relationships with exponents of the court and even with family members of his persecutor Hideyoshi, but above all he never stopped fighting, carving out new spaces for maneuver in the court thanks to his skills as a warrior.[26] In short, Ukon was fully immersed in the events of his time and paid a high price for fidelity to Catholicism, yet he remained a warrior, ready to shed blood for political reasons as well as for his God. The complexity of this figure, split between service of the sword and devotion to the cross, was to some extent nurtured by Ukon himself – if indeed, after being reconciled, katana in hand, with Hideyoshi, he was keen to write to Valignano to reiterate that "with all these favors, he remains devoted" and that

> he would desire to lead a private and withdrawn life much more than to return to take over the management of governments again, and to stay in court, and that out of respect for his wife, son and relatives could not put into effect his good wishes, yet on the whole he felt consoled by seeing himself free from the toil and danger in which he had been living.[27]

A testimony following his death, written in Macao by a Jesuit missionary, leads us in the same direction. It deals extensively with the passing away of Ukon and the impact of the news not only on the priests who remained in the archipelago, but also on the faithful and his enemies.[28] Unpublished details emerged on the sumptuous welcome received by the Christian daimyo and his followers upon their arrival in Manila by the ecclesiastical and political authorities, but also by "the whole city that came to meet him, came out of jubilation as if to thank him," but above all on the funeral which "they say was such as Manila has never seen," both for the unprecedented duration of eight whole days "with a sea of people in ebb and flow," and for the "signs of pain and common feeling of the loss of such a great man," and again for the generosity of the Spanish viceroy who assigned rents to the descendants of

Ukon and to the other exiles for their faith so they could support themselves. However, the announcement of the Christian daimyo's death also struck the highest Japanese authorities, and in particular Tokugawa Ieyasu, who – again according to the Jesuit missionary – "showed his regret at having lost such an able soldier and rider, and says he praised his generosity and brains." Yet until the end he had considered him a formidable opponent, capable of subverting the balance of the war in Osaka against Hideyoshi's heir, and therefore had ordered his assassination before his departure for Manila. Ukon, on the other hand, had managed – according to the Jesuits – to leave the Japanese coasts before the arrival of the assassins, having now turned his "heartfelt thoughts toward exile for the love of Christ." In this way he had missed the appointment with martyrdom, but only to access a different degree of beatification:

> God willed that the good Justo should surpass his fame with the presence of his heroic virtues, which accomplished in a death if not of blood, then at least with a long martyrdom, since without any doubt his death was hastened with the exile.[29]

## A martyr without martyrdom

From December 1616, a few months after Ukon's death, a particular profile of the saint and martyr was elaborated in the circles of the Jesuit mission in the Far East, by now split between Macao, Manila and Japan, which insisted on some salient moments and certain aspects not always taken for granted in his biography, with the already manifest intention of constructing a functional image of him for the canonization process to be submitted to Rome. The wholly singular concept of "long martyrdom" achieved without bloodshed, for example, appeared from then on and was systematically taken up again until the recent beatification. Also in 1616, another Jesuit, the aforementioned Matheo de Couros, emphasized how the death of Ukon, without shedding any blood had in no way caused the loss of the "palmam martyrii,"[30] deserved instead for having suffered so long because of his faith during exile: "With such a death that, although he did not shed his blood, we can rightly say that he did not lose the palm of martyrdom, due solely to exile."[31]

In these testimonies shortly after his death, if it is true that the military and political dimension of the character still found space, the image of Ukon was, however, not yet completely fixed. The most significant example is offered by the *Relacíon del suceso que tuvo nuestra santa fe en los Reinos del Japón* by the Portuguese Jesuit Luis Piñeiro, published in 1617 in Madrid. The volume first of all set out to defend the Society's work in Japan from the defamatory accusations launched by the Franciscans and other competing orders, demonstrating how their pastoral action complied perfectly with the Tridentine decrees, also in matters of the cult of relics and veneration of saints. Secondly, it pursued the objective of aligning the Jesuit presence in the Far East with the political and commercial interests of the Spanish crown in the Pacific, thus releasing them from their overly close ties with Portugal.[32]

In this sense, the enhancement of the arrival in Manila, in the Spanish Philippines, of Japanese exiles, including Ukon, acquired a particular meaning.[33] Piñeiro underscored the majestic welcome offered by the Spanish authorities of the island,[34] the fact that the figure of the Christian daimyo was already known to the governor,[35] who, in addition to paying him great honors, offered him pensions from the crown (refused by Ukon)[36] and, in the days following his arrival, repeatedly spent time with him to discuss matters of state and war.[37] In the Portuguese Jesuit's text, the political dimension of the future blessed was fully valued, for example, by highlighting the appreciation of the daimyo – as a valiant and expert swordsman – with blanks fired by the arquebusiers in his honor.[38] But certainly even more significant were the references to his past as a man of arms by Ukon himself in the speech he gave to his relatives on his deathbed. To demonstrate the transience of earthly events and to invite his wife and children to entrust themselves exclusively to the Lord rather than men, the old daimyo recalled the years spent in the service of the emperors and shoguns of Japan, for whom he had fought valiantly, unsheathing his katana without holding back, and wore armor more often than silk clothes, to the point of seeing his beard whiten under the helmet in all those decades of faithful militancy. And yet, he concluded with bitterness, despite that irreproachable loyalty, he had been most persecuted by precisely those whom he had served the most.[39]

Previously however, in presenting the figure of Ukon to the reader, at the time of his expulsion from Kanazawa in 1614, at the beginning of the long journey of exile which then culminated with his arrival in Manila, the author had placed the "great value of his faith" and the "significant feats performed by him in war at the time of Nobunaga and Hideyoshi."[40] In that case too, the most revealing passage was a speech put into Ukon's mouth when he was leaving the city to instill courage in his family members forced to endure the hard test of exile: the metaphor used was indeed warlike, and recalled the battlefield in which the gaze of the commander, whose eyes instilled strength and determination in the soldiers, was often decisive. In the same way it was necessary to turn our gaze to Christ, the only true lord of Christians, capable of giving courage in those painful situations to exiles destined to lose everything in the name of their faith, yet journeying toward the crown of martyrdom.[41] Piñeiro's approach was no different in the concluding pages dedicated to a summary recapitulation of Ukon's life. Here, too, his involvement in the wars and political transactions of his time was far from minimized, his stature as a valiant leader at the service of the great unifiers of Japan was, on several occasions, reiterated, and his fidelity to the faith of the Gospel made him, in the eyes of the Portuguese Jesuit, not an ascetic alien to the world, but a model of life against the tide among men without betraying his moral and religious principles, a sort of *miles christianus* with almond-shaped eyes, a model for the warriors of the Land of the Rising Sun, but also for the gentlemen of old Christian Europe.[42] As in other sources, it extolled the participation of Ukon and other converted leaders' crusader soldiers from among the ranks of Hideyoshi's army on the occasion of the conquest of Kyushu in 1587.[43] Similarly there was no lack of explicit praise for his military talent,[44] which ended up constituting a fundamental element in the construction of the post-mortem identity of the Japanese daimyo, who had risen to a lay model of a soldier of Christ fully integrated into the aristocratic society of sixteenth-seventeenth-century Japan.

Only later – and in line with the methodological orientation of the first Jesuit historiography[45] – was a selective memory imposed which archived the conflictual and somewhat inconsistent dimension of the future blessed, in favor of the linear biographical portrait of a living saint, ready to abandon political manipulations and military commitments from his youth to embrace a sober and exemplary life of prayer. And such is the Ukon that we find under the pen of his confessor and fellow exile Pedro Morejón, who had had the opportunity to see him in his last years in Kanazawa, had guided him in his spiritual exercises in Nagasaki shortly before setting sail for Manila, and had heard his confession one last time on his deathbed. He therefore must have known in depth the old daimyo's soul, secrets and past – and, as such, became the main architect his transformation into an aspiring saint. The Philippine authorities asked him to write a biography of Ukon, which remained in manuscript and in all probability is now lost, but from which Morejón drew heavily to complete other works.

From the summer of 1615, before leaving Manila, the Jesuit had been completing the draft of his *Relacion de la persecucion que vuo en la yglesia de Japon*, in which, among the many events concerning Christian Japan he recounted to the world's faithful, he dwelt quite extensively on Takayama, outlining the first complete biography. As often happened to Spanish missionaries returning to Europe, instead of going through Asia and Africa, the Jesuit undertook the reverse path, crossing the Pacific Ocean and landing in Mexico, where the first edition of the work saw the light.[46] It confirmed the existence of a missionary Catholicism not without its own originality, straddling the Pacific, circulating men and texts that triangulated Europe, the Spanish possessions of Central and South America, and Asia, with the Philippines, Japan and the eastern coast of China.[47] It was precisely to those faithful recently converted to Catholicism that Morejón first chose to address the proposal of a lay saint, especially a non-European like Takayama, who could echo the simultaneous attempt to beatify Rose of Lima, the Dominican tertiary of Peruvian origins,[48] which was crowned with success, despite the initial intervention of the Inquisition. The following year, having arrived in the Old Continent, the last confessor of Ukon printed a second version of his work in Zaragoza, almost identical to the first, if not for a significant expansion of the biographical profile of the Japanese daimyo who was candidate for the altars.[49]

In retracing Ukon's earthly trajectory, Morejón insisted on some crucial moments in his embracing Christianity: the conversion, which took place under the guidance of his father Dario in the distant 1560s; and the role played by the Takayama clan in protecting the Jesuit missionaries; and then the role of Ukon himself as a propagator of the Gospel, both among the subjects of his fiefdoms and at court. But the heart of the biographical story were three tests of his faith in Christ, which resumed his approach toward the altars already elaborated in the reports sent in previous years from Japan, when Ukon was still alive. The first turning point was in fact the siege of the Takatsuki fortress, during which Takayama's loyalty passed from Araki to Nobunaga, when he did not hesitate to defend the missionaries, jeopardizing his own honor and sacrificing his own children, like "another Abraham" who "decided to die in the world." The second key moment was the ban of 1587 by Hideyoshi, which led to the effective renunciation – in reality only temporary, though Morejón preferred to gloss over this point – of political aspirations along with all temporal goods, and his condemnation to a life of wandering. The third moment was the exile of 1614 and his departure for Manila, "he was always waiting for death, so cheerful, and peaceful" ("siempre estuuo esperando por la muerte, tan alegre, y quieto"). Then the notion of a prolonged martyrdom ("martirio prolongado") reappeared, as we have already seen suggested in some missionary letters, which was identified with exile ("destierro") rather than with a grisly death.

The focus placed on those three moments were all interpreted in relation to the Society and in an exclusively religious logic. Unlike Piñeiro – who speaks of "three battles" rather than trials, and, as we have seen, does not keep silent about Ukon's involvement in political negotiations and the military[50] – Morejón could put aside the political and military experience that Ukon had engaged in not only under Nobunaga and Hideyoshi, but also between the late sixteenth and early seventeenth centuries under the Tokugawa. In the same way, the author downplays the political trajectory of his father Dario, whose fall from grace came by the will of the Odas rather than his own choice.[51] He also makes small propaedeutic exaggerations to depict Ukon as a samurai of Christ, by then far from the internal wars of his time, the pure figure of a man who had turned his back on the century under the guidance of the missionary priests. This image of a devoted daimyo, intent on spreading Christianity by his own example, but also through the destruction of Buddhist temples and the expulsion of bonzes from his lands to make way for the building of churches and the raising of large crosses,[52] spread through the press in America and Europe. It was presented again by the Jesuit before those responsible for the process of canonization of Japanese martyrs, including Ukon initially, on October 5, 1630 when he gave his testimony in Manila.[53] The impossibility of conducting the preliminary investigation in the archipelago due to the exacerbation of persecutions and the expulsion of all the missionaries slowed down the beatification process to the point of blocking it in the following years.

Nonetheless, other texts took up the story of Ukon as an example of someone converted to the Christian faith, re-launching the image of an aspiring martyr destined for the altars. In 1650 the Jesuit Antonio Francisco Cardim published in Lisbon the *Elogios e ramalhete de flores borrifado com o sangue dosligios da Companhia de Iesu, a quem os tyrannos do Imperio de Iappaõ tiraraõ as vidas por odio da Fè Catholica*, to which was attached a *Catalogo de todos os religiosos et seculares, que por odio da mesma Fè foraõ mortos naquelle Imperio atê o anno de 1640*. Through that calendar of martyrs and saints *in pectore* – which, however, still lacked Rome's approval – Ukon also established himself as a reference figure for missionary Catholicism. In the chapter dedicated to him, the three episodes already at the center of Morejón's biography were taken up again, exalting his vocation to martyrdom, always faced with "very cheerful and considerate face," parallels were made with ancient heroes such as Hannibal or Alexander the Great, and he was proclaimed a true column of the Japanese Church, according to a formula already used by previous authors. The image that accompanied the biographical lines was, if possible, even more explicit in recalling the now dominant interpretation of Christ's samurai who had chosen to drop his weapons, helmet and shield to embrace a large wooden cross. Cardim's brief summary then concluded with the explicit wish for an imminent beatification by the Church of Rome: "Waiting for the Roman Church to declare us Martyrs who suffered so much for her."[54]

The year 1663 saw the publication of *Labor evangelica, ministerios apostolicos de los obreros de la Compania de Iesus, fundacion, y progressos de su. Provincia en las islas filipinas*,[55] a work by another Jesuit, Francisco Colin, dedicated to the mission in the Philippines in which ample prominence was given to the Japanese daimyo who came to die in the capital of the island.[56] The entire chapter XXVIII was in fact dedicated to the *Relacion compendiosa de la vida, hechos, y virtudes del Ilustre Cavallero, y Confessor de Christo Don Iusto Catayama. Vulgarmente llamado Ucandono*, in which the author, by his own admission, took from previous biographies, in particular those of Guzman and Morejón, whose work he had been able to consult published in Mexico in 1616, but also the manuscript life of Ukon now lost.[57] This demonstrates the circulation of those texts, published or in manuscript, within the area of Christianity in the Pacific Ocean, and the direct construction of a collective memory on the events and protagonists of the Catholicization of the Far East.[58] It is therefore not surprising that the overall interpretation follows the biographical approach elaborated by the last Jesuit confessor. In fact, even in the *Labor evangelica* the three fundamental moments of Ukon's life recur as essential stages around which the holy samurai's entire spiritual path revolved. And as in the previous biographies, a decisive nexus was established between the suffering in his last years due to persecution and exile, his death in Manila, and his legitimate definition as martyr, despite the lack of a violent death.[59]

However, since it was a sort of collage from several sources (some of which are not known today), probably including the pages of Piñeiro, Colin's work was less focused, and left room, here and there, for original annotations, in particular regarding to Takayama's participation in military campaigns on behalf of Maeda Toshiie, and therefore indirectly also for Hideyoshi, in the last part of the sixteenth century[60] as well as to the request, which arrived a few days after his departure for Manila, still in 1614 by Hideyoshi's son to take part in the defense of Osaka against the Tokugawa.[61] In describing his arrival in Manila, the author insisted on the solemn welcome granted him by the Spanish authorities of the Philippines, in particular by the governor who had spoken with him "long hours" about "things from Japan" since

> Don Justo had always been raised at Court, and had handled the greatest matters of state, in peace and war, and he had such great judgment, he answered the Governor's questions so accurately, that every day he became more fond of him.[62]

Even more interesting was Colin's text when it dealt with the funeral of Ukon in which the entire city had participated, just as the annotations on the already very lively cult of the future blessed – whom he repeatedly called "holy man" and martyr – on the part of the faithful, eager to come and "kiss his feet, like Saint Martyr."[63] But to venerate the daimyo as already raised to the altars, despite the prohibitions imposed in the same years by the Church of Rome, Colin emphasized, were not only the lay faithful, "but also the same greatly edifying religious devotion which the Japanese admired." As such, it was living cult, that of Takayama, somewhat spontaneous, but immediately managed by the Jesuit priests interested in building a profile of missionary holiness in those lands very far from Rome. Not even twenty years later, the well-informed Colin noted, Ukon's corpse was moved from the old Church of the Jesuit College to that of the seminary of San José; and on the occasion the fathers chose to "separate the bones of such an illustrious man, and martyr of Christ from the others, and put them in a well-adorned drawer in the interior Chapel of the College, with a brush portrait of him on top."[64]

## The post-mortem career: from failures to the altars

As such, in the Philippines during the early months of 1615, there was already a spontaneous cult of Christ's samurai, considered a holy martyr who died for his fidelity to the Gospel. Although his life was spent in close ties with the Society of Jesus, his exile and death in Manila, territory subject to the Spaniards, made him interesting for the reconstruction of relations between the crown of Spain and the Jesuits, by now expelled from the archipelago; it also transformed him into a figure of global missionary Catholicism, and therefore exploitable by other religious orders as well, such as the Franciscans and the Dominicans.[65] Handwritten and printed hagiographies of Takayama soon circulated, which experienced worldwide diffusion on the initiative of the Society of Jesus. Despite its lay status, Takayama did not cease to legitimately claim a special bond with that candidate to the altars.[66] The highest honors and exceptional treatment were reserved for his corpse, with the placement of the tomb in the internal chapel under an image of him. Very soon it became an object of worship by the faithful. In addition to kissing the feet and hands of the deceased amid the fragrance of sanctity,[67] the numerous faithful who flocked to pay him their last homage fought for shreds of his clothes to make precious relics.[68] As has been said, these cult practices were widespread and recurring in Catholicism in the modern age, so is therefore not surprising to see them reappear as such even in the context of the missionary Church. Yet, precisely in the same years in which men like Piñeiro, Morejón or Colin promoted the cult of the Japanese daimyo in the Pacific Ocean, from the Philippines to the Mexican coasts of New Spain, in Rome the papacy sanctioned an epochal turning point regarding the process of beatification and canonization, through the publication of some decrees which, point by point, contradicted those forms of sanctification from below.[69]

In 1625 a decree forbade any type of public and private worship of anyone who died with a reputation for holiness without the explicit authorization of the Apostolic See. Two years later it was established that to start a process of beatification it was necessary that at least 50 years had passed since the death of the candidate for the halo and that no public cult had developed in the meantime. In 1634 another decree established the need for each canonization to start a particular process, called *super non cultu*, in order to ascertain that in fact there was no previous type of veneration.[70] For several years, however, the rule had been imposed according to which there should be neither lives nor portraits of saintly candidates that depicted them as such, just as spontaneous forms of worship had been prohibited on the occasion of funerals. These stringent rules, aimed to limit and direct the way of conceiving and living holiness in early seventeenth-century Europe, caused a block in the canonization processes already started, in particular by the Society of Jesus, which did not fit into that new regulatory system. Yet it maintained its own alternative and original approach to holiness, despite the guidelines of the Holy Office which were soon adopted by the papacy.

This, therefore, explains the failure of the repeated attempts to promote the Japanese warrior to the honors of the altars, exactly as happened with such better-known and titled figures as Roberto Bellarmino or Pietro Canisio, who only completed their process in the twentieth century. With those other Jesuit saints, Takayama Ukon shared certain characteristics; that is, he adapted to a very specific typology: he was the expression of an effort to understand and adapt to a local context, which was, however, very distant and different from the Europe of the modern age, able to turn to new communities of converts, in particular to the feudal aristocracy of the Japanese archipelago who recognized in that warrior of God one of their own, although converted to the new faith. In this sense he was truly the concrete representation of Valignano's *accomodatio*. It was a project of temporary coexistence with other cults and other religions, to which the idea of persecution and martyrdom in blood remained extraneous. Finally, he was a living saint, perceived as such by his contemporaries, and immediately represented in this way in the first hagiographies and missionary letters: that is, a man who could serve as an ethical and virtuous model of behavior, devoid of any magical or thaumaturgical dimension, capable of seducing with his spirit of charity and capacity to love his neighbor, rather than for his miracles,[71] according to a line promoted by the Spanish current of the order headed by Pedro de Ribadeneira.[72] And thus we understand the eighteenth-century success of the story of Ukon in the theater of Jesuit colleges throughout Europe, where he was presented precisely for the purpose of edifying and training future missionaries.[73]

On the other hand, the model that was imposed in Rome in the seventeenth century was different, where despite internal resistance the Church ended up favoring models of devotion centered on miracles and a concept of martyrdom understood in a restrictive sense: that is, directly connected to bloody death at the hands of infidels. As such, the model of local holiness and prolonged martyrdom of which Ukon was the perfect expression lost all interest for the Roman hierarchies: a model by now surpassed in theory and practice by the Church of the Counter-Reformation. But there must have been other critical issues that prevented the Japanese daimyo from a rapid ascent to the altars. In a time of strengthening the distinction and separation between clergy and laity, Ukon was the expression of a devout laity, substantially autonomous from ecclesiastical authorities. Moreover, he was not a missionary who left for the Indies, but a non-European man converted to the Catholic faith, and therefore, culturally distant, which was not as suitable to the devotion of European novices and faithful.

It is no coincidence that in the numerous writings dedicated to the memory of the mission in Japan, missionaries of European or South American origin were privileged for a long time, while little or no space was granted to Japanese converts, who had also died by the hundreds during the persecutions.[74] Finally, a basic contradiction remained unresolved, namely the social role of Ukon, who, as we have seen, never ceased to be a warrior, influential on a political and military level; while aspiring to shed his own blood for Christ, he had never stopped shedding the blood of others on the battlefields of Japan's protracted civil war of the sixteenth and seventeenth centuries. To these reasons must be added questions of a practical nature: namely, the insurmountable difficulty for the Roman Church and its departments to exercise effective control over such distant territories, where there was no longer even a bishop capable of certifying the various steps of the canonization process and to complete the collection of local testimonies.[75]

And yet, this missionary sanctity, due to the urgency of its bearing witness to a persecuted and living faith, escaped the cage of rules and norms imposed by Rome. It did not take fifty years to see the cult of the blessed candidate flourish, opposing with irreducible resistance the abstract, coldly controlled models of sainthood. This also explains the survival of Japanese Christianity despite centuries of closure and persecution, and the vitality of the cult of Christ's samurai, still on the threshold of the new millennium, both in the archipelago and in the Philippines. As such, the reasons that explain the failure of Takayama's candidacy throughout the modern age help instead to understand the success achieved four centuries later, when precisely those distinctive elements of a secular, local and in many ways original sanctity with respect to the Tridentine models ended up appealing to the Church of the third millennium, interested in promoting cults aimed at non-European faithful, and legitimately eager to identify themselves with men and women perceived as belonging to their history and their culture.

There is substantially no trace of this reversal trend nor of these inextricable contradictions in the documentation collected on the occasion of the resumption of the beatification process starting from the 1960s, on the initiative of the archdiocese of Osaka, and then culminating in 1971 with the ordinary information gathering process. Instead, those papers limited themselves to the profile and overall interpretation Ukon as traced by his first seventeenth-century biographers. Not surprisingly, they chose not to use Piñeiro's *Relación*, which, despite its wealth of information, presented the figure of Ukon as too involved in earthly affairs.[76] The three decisive moments of his journey of faith are thus emphasized, and the concept of martyrdom in duration, without bloodshed, is recovered based on a distinction between "formal martyrdom" and "material martyrdom"[77] and inspired by the example of Francis Xavier, who had also suffered an "interior martyrdom."[78] In this sense, according to the postulators of his cause, Ukon learned to understand and then lived a form of "superior martyrdom," which does not "mean causing violent death, almost like hara-kiri, thinking that it is the result of human decision alone," but rather freeing himself "from the mistaken trust in one's own abilities."[79] An itinerary therefore from Peter to Job, during which the blessed samurai was able to experience the "difference between the active desire for martyrdom and being passively exposed to conditions that only slowly lead to death," i.e. a prolonged martyrdom, which allows full Christological identification with participation "in the impotence of the Lord nailed to the cross."[80]

In the same way, the idea of an ethical model of holiness is valued since the Japanese warrior, in an age of unbridled ambitions and great upheavals, had known how not to let himself be "snared by the allure of power, glory and money."[81] Despite an appreciable effort of documentary collection, the historical figure of Ukon remains on the margins; his political and military role continues to be diminished in favor of the all-round saintly image, free from smudges and contradictions, of a devout layman persecuted to the point of his death in exile in Manila. For obvious strategic reasons of compliance with rules still in force, the burning problem of the existence of a cult of the future blessed is ignored from the moment of death; yet there is still the *super non cultu* investigation in which some witnesses are asked if there had been in the centuries following his disappearance some form of spontaneous devotion toward the samurai of Christ.[82] In reality, an early cult of Ukon existed as evident to anyone who has looked through the numerous contemporary testimonies provided by the Jesuits themselves or, more simply, traveled, as this writer has, before the beatification of 2017 to Nagasaki, Takayama, Takatsuki or Kanazawa, where in the squares and especially in the churches one could already admire various types of statues, paintings and representations of Ukon, characteristic of a saint and martyr.

The case of Takayama Ukon, therefore, proves to be useful for reflecting on the ability of the Church of Rome to adapt to the times of history, and on its undeniable ability to contradict itself without any retractions over the centuries. At the time of his death and the first failed attempts at beatification at the beginning of the seventeenth century, the case of the Japanese daimyo, in fact, represented a model that had been overcome by events. After the experience of building Christianity in the Japanese archipelago exhausted itself, his model of prolonged martyrdom was ill suited to a combative and triumphant Counter-Reformation, in need of holy martyrs willing to die as warriors rather than warriors who lived and died as holy martyrs. Only centuries later, with changed power relations within Catholicism – all the more following the accession to the Petrine throne of a Jesuit pope originally from the New World, who in his youth wanted to be a missionary in Japan – did Takayama's sanctification regain momentum, despite the residual critical issues and unresolved contradictions. Yet his case also demonstrates to us the complexity and diversity of Catholicism in the modern age. It was capable of formulating internally, especially in the peripheral extra-European missions, models and instances of holiness and martyrdom in competition – if not outright contradiction – with each other, despite a desire on the part of the Roman center to standardize attitudes and practices to a single typology through the imposition of decrees and norms.

## Notes

1 Gotor, *I beati del papa*, cit., pp. 43–126.
2 Sergio Luzzatto, *Padre Pio. Miracoli e politica nell'Italia del Novecento*, Torino, Einaudi, 2007, p. 9; Fabietti, *Materia sacra*, cit., pp. 57–60.
3 «Al toque de las campanas, que en muriendo se hizo, fue tan grande el dolor en toda la ciudad, como sia cada uno se le muriera persona que mucho amava. Es

possible, dezian, que murio a quel Santo, no mereciamos gozar mas del no huvo en la ciudad, por buen espacio otra platica, sino de Iusto, de su virtud, de su prduencia, y juyzio, de su muerte, del entierro, y honras que se le devian hazer, todos se le hazian predicadores» (Piñeiro, *Relacíon del suceso que tuvo nuestra santa fe en los Reinos del Japón*, cit., p. 350).

4 Gotor, *Chiesa e santità nell'Italia moderna*, cit., pp. 54–66. On Roman attempts to regulate devotional acts on the occasion of funerals of the deceased in the fragrance of sanctity cf. Gotor, *I beati del papa*, cit., pp. 149–51.

5 On the role of Morejón in the process of beatification of the Nagasaki 26 and for the recent bibliography on him cf. Omata Rappo, *Des Indes lointaines aux scènes des collèges*, cit., pp. 142–45; Eduardo Javier Alonso Romo, *Pedro Morejón: vida, obra e itinerario transoceánico de un jesuita castellano*, in Martínez Millán, Pizarro Llorente, Jiménez Pablo (ed.), *Los jesuitas. Religión, política y educación (siglos XVI–XVIII)*, cit., vol. 3, pp. 1559–72.

6 Gotor, *I beati del papa*, cit., pp. 275–84.

7 Ucerler, *The Samurai and the Cross*, cit., p. 29.

8 On the conversion of Dario cf. Giovan Pietro Maffei, *Le historie delle Indie orientali*, In Venetia, appresso Damian Zenaro, 1589, p. 400 rv.

9 Valignano, *Sumario de las cosas de Japon (1583)*, cit., pp. 124–25, 277.

10 See bibliography cited in chap. 1.

11 Ucerler, *The Samurai and the Cross*, cit., pp. 191–200.

12 Michael Cooper (ed.), *They Came to Japan. An anthology of European Reports on Japan, 1543–1640*, Ann Arbor, The University of Michigan, Center for Japanese studies, 1995 (1965), p. 136.

13 Fróis, *Historia de Japam*, cit., ad indicem.

14 "Questa christianità ha per capo un signore christiano chiamato Giusto, persona molto signalata e di gran stima in quel regno, et molto buon christiano" (*Alcune lettere delle cose del Giappone. Scritte da' reverendi padri della Compagnia di Iesu. Dell'anno 1579 insino al 1581*, Roma, Francesco Zanetti, 1584, pp. 66–67).

15 Ivi, pp. 66–72.

16 "pericolo certo di perdere lo stato e la vita" (*Lettera annale del Giappone scritta al padre generale della Compagnia di Giesù alli XX febraio M.D.L.XXXXVIII*, in Roma, appresso Francesco Zannetti, 1590, p. 59).

17 "In questa sua partenza non li pregava né instantemente li domandava altro, se non che fossero forti et costanti nella Fede insino al spargere il sangue, et dare la vita per quella; et che vivessero come buoni Christiani, dando di loro quel essempio di virtù, ch'havevano sempre dato, come sperava et confidava di loro" (Ivi, p. 58).

18 "in habito et stato molto differente da quello in che prima eravamo soliti di vederlo [...] in habito molto positivo, sconosciuto et come peregrino con sei soli servidori, quali anco egli trattava come compagni, conducendoli seco copertamente. [...] honore e di robba [...] andava però meno contento et alegro" (*Lettere del Giappone et della Cina degl'anni M.D.LXXXIX & M.D.XC scritte al R.P. Generale della Compagnia di Giesù*, in Milano, per Pacifico Pontio, 1592, pp. 49–50).

19 Ivi, p. 54.

20 "Tutto il popolo, sino le donne e i fanciulli l'honoravano et riverivano grandemente, correva appresso a vederlo ogni sorte di gente, occupando le strade, dove egli passava in modo che a pena a lui restava luogo per passare avanti: et tutti applaudendogli attorno, et facendo maravigliosa festa della sua venuta: predicavano la sua virtù, laudavano la forteza dell'animo, la constante sua pietà" (ivi, p. 50).

21 "patienza et l'allegrezza con che egli persevera in sostenere questo essilio con tanti travagli, et povertà propria, e di casa sua, vivendo in essi un continuo desiderio di versare anco il sangue et dar la vita per Christo" (ivi, p. 51).

22 "Giusto Ucondono, sì come per il passato è stato sempre un raro specchio d'ogni virtù a tutta questa Chiesa, così ancora nelle divotione, e nel zelo dell'honor di Dio

è il principal sostegno c'habbino quei christiani, insegnando, e aiutando tutti, né mai perde occasione di tirar quanti più può al conoscimento del vero Dio; d'onde nasce, che col suo zelo si va multiplicando ogni dì più, e perfettionando quella Christianità" (*Tre lettere annue del Giappone, degli anni 1603, 1604, 1605 e parte del 1606*, In Bologna, Appresso Gio. Battista Bellagamba, 1609, p. 60).

23 Ivi, pp. 123–24. For Ukon's similar commitment to proselytism, see also *Lettera annua di Giappone, scritta nel 1601 e mandata dal P. Francesco Pasio V. Provinciale*, in Roma, appresso Luigi Zannetti, 1603, pp. 63–65.

24 See for example Luis de Guzman, *Historia de las missiones que han hecho los religiosos dela Compania de Iesus, para predicar el sancto Evangelio en la India Oriental, y en los Reynos de la China y Japon*, en Alcala, por la Biuda de Juan Gracian, 1601, vol. 2, p. 331. On Guzman see Roldán-Figueroa, *The Martyrs of Japan*, cit., pp. 145–96.

25 Giovanni Botero in *Le Relationi universali* (1591), mentions the case of the convert Ukon several times (Giovanni Botero, *Le relazioni universali*, a cura di Blythe Alice Raviola, Torino, Nino Aragno Editore, 2015–2017, vol. 2, pp. 1045–48).

26 *Lettera del Giappone degli anni 1591 et 1592, scritta al R.P. Generale della Compagnia di Giesù*, In Roma, appresso Luigi Zanetti, 1595, pp. 133–36.

27 "con tutti questi favori, egli resta[va] tanto divoto […] desiderarebbe di far vita particolare e ritirata più assai che tornar a pigliar di nuovo i maneggi de' governi, et a star in corte, et che se bene per rispetto di sua moglie, figliuolo e parenti non poteva mandare ad effetto i suoi buoni desiderii, si consolava con tutto ciò di vedersi libero dal travaglio, e pericolo nel quale già viveva" (ivi, p. 135). Still on the eve of his definitive exile from Japan, the shogunal authorities feared his political and military influence (cf. Morejón's beautiful letter contained in *Lettera annua del Giappone del M.DC.XIV al molto reverendo padre Mutio Vitelleschi, generale della Compagnia di Giesù*, in Roma, Per Bartolomeo Zannetti, 1617, pp. 63–74).

28 On the importance of the moment of death in Jesuit culture cf. Michela Catto, *La scena pubblica della morte. L'istante ultimo e il compimento della vocazione gesuitica*, in «Rivista storica italiana», CXXXII/3 (2020), pp. 1068–85.

29 "tutta la città che lo venne ad incontrare, uscivano di giubilo come di se e non finivano di renderne gratie […] dicono essere state tali quali non ha veduto mai Maniglia […] con un mare di popolo in flusso e riflusso, […] segnali del dolore e sentimento comune della perdita d'un tanto grand'huomo, […] ha mostro dispiacere dell'esser mancato un huomo in arme et in maneggio tanto segnalato, e si dice che ha lodato la generosità e cervello di lui. […] Di cuore il pensiero ad andare in esilio per l'amor di Cristo. […] Volle Iddio che il buon Giusto superasse la fama che di lui correva con la presenza dell'heroiche virtù sue, le quali egli smaltò in morte se non col suo sangue, almeno col lungo martirio, essendosegli senz'alcun dubbio con l'esiglio accelerata la morte" (*Lettere annue del Giappone, China, Goa et Ethiopia, scritte al M.R.P. Generale della Compagnia di Giesù, dai padri dell'istessa Compagnia negli anni 1615, 1617, 1618, 1619*, in Napoli, Per Lazaro Scoriggio, 1621, pp. 91–93).

30 Letters of Matheo de Couros, Nagasaki, 15 March 1616, in ARSI, Jap. Sin. 58, f. 333v.

31 "con una muerte tal que, auque no derramó su sangre, podemos decir con razón que no perdió la palma del martirio, debida únicamente al destierro" (Juan G. Ruiz de Medina (ed.), *El martirologio del Japón: 1558–1873*, Roma, Institutum Historicum Societatis Iesu, 1999, p. 356).

32 Piñeiro, *Relacíon del suceso que tuvo nuestra santa fe en los Reinos del Japón*, cit., pp. 206–9.

33 "He aqui a Iusto, despues de aver servido a tantos Reynos, mudado tantos estados, peregrinado por tantas tierras, muerto ultimamente con tanta felicidad en las de la Catolica corona de nuestra España, que parece quiso Dios nuestro Señor coronar en ella sua santa, y illustre vida" (Ivi, p. 353).

34 Ivi, pp. 342–47.
35 "Luego que en Manilla se supo llegava el navio de los desterrados, siervos de Dios, se sintio en toda la ciudad una alegria universal, desseando hazerles unas grandes fiestas, particularmente el governador don Iuan da Silva que tenia mucha noticia de don Iusto" (Ivi, p. 344).
36 "Al mismo Padre encarecidamente encargò que en ningun modo se tratasse de renta, porque gustava tanto de aver dexado por la Fè laque tenia, que le seria desconsuelo topar con otras, y con ocasiones de pensar que Dios no le aceptava lo que le avia ofrecido; y que bien sabia el, que conforme al pundonor de la cavalleria de Iapon, no podia admitir renta sin servicio; y pues no estava y a en estado de poder servir a su Magestad, ni a su Señoria, en ningun modo se tratasse della, porque no la avia de aceptar" (Ivi, p. 346).
37 "El governador no contento de embiarle luego avisitar con un rico presente, y muy a proposito, fue en persona averle a su casa, y porque no se hartava de hablar con el, venia al Colegio casi todos los dias, donde gastava con Iusto largas horas, preguntandole muchas cosas del estado y govierno, de la paz, y guerra, y como Iusto desde sus primeros annos se avia criado en la corte y usado siempre las armas, y principalmente por ser hombre de muy buen juyzio, satisfazia a todo tan formal, y puntualmente, que se admirava el Governador y cada dia crecia la opinion que del avia cobrado, holgose mucho en que ya que tal hombre huuiesse de salir desterrado de su estado, viniesse a Manilla, y teniase por dichoso de estar en esta ocasion en aquel govierno" (Ivi, p. 346).
38 "Al entrar de la puerta del muro les estavan aguardando gran numero de arcabuzeros, todos auna dispararon con mucha presteza, haziendo una bonissima salva, de la qual don Iusto, como hombre exercitado en armas, mostrò gran gusto, alabando la destreza de los Españoles" (Ivi, pp. 344–45).
39 "O quantas mas vezes se mudan las esperanças del mundo que el vedor del campo. Basteos por exemplo vuestro padre; la barba me apuntò y encaneciò debaxo del yelmo; mas vezes vesti malla de azero, que ropa de seda, nunca mi catana saltò en ocasion alguna de importancia, y siempre fue de las mas corradoras en servicio de mis emperadores, y con todo esso testifica el mundo, que fuy perseguido de los que mejor he servido" (Ivi, pp. 348–49).
40 "Figendono [...] tenia por capitanes insignes algunos christianos, y sobre todos a don Iusto, que passava ya de los sesenta, muy conocido en las historias del Iapon, con nombre de Iusto Ucondono, assi por el gran valor de su Fe, como por las insignes proezas que hizo en la guerras, en tiempo del Emperador Nobunanga, y Taycosama" (Ivi, pp. 258–59).
41 "Caminando este tercio de gente tan luzida, yua entre ellos Iusto, como padre, y caudillo de todos animandolos, como hombre mas auentajado, en autoridad, y esfuerço: una vezes, como capitan a soldados, les dezia. Ea pues desterrados por Christo, los esforçados tienen el mundo por patria, los reales por salas, el trabajo por sustento quando nos veamos en el mas riguroso destierro por su santo nombre, entonces estamos en mas dulce patria, en mas doradas salas, en regalo mas suave. Si en la guerra acostunbrava mos andar con el oydo atento a la voz de nuestro capitan, para obedecerle, agora caminemos, poniendo la mira en nuestro Christo para imitarle; y aunque el animo de todos està prometiendo la perseverancia necessaria para la corona, asseguralda, arrimando lo que en vos ay lo mucho que Dio puede. Si ponemos los ojos en Dios, Dios los pondra en nosotros, y con esso quedara nuestro trabajo de mas estima; si en la batallas, y occasiones de merecer los ojos de los reyes esengendran espiritus en los animos, ponen fuerça en los braços, y dan precio a los servicios de sus vassallos, los divinos que tal lo daran a los vuestro? [...] Pues caminemos alegremente a las espaldas queda el miedo, adelante va la corona" (Ivi, pp. 262–63).

42 "Puesto en medio del fuego de Babilonia, fue tan notoria su limpieza, y honestidad de vida, que el mismo Taycosama [Hideyoshi] le loava desta virtud, como de cosa rara y maravillosa, y muchos senores de la corte convencidos de la hermosura della y de la verdad de los sermones, reconocian la eminencia de nuestra santa ley, y afirmaron no se bautizavan porque no podrian vivir castamente assi como Iusto, no es (dezian) de hombre noble y honrado professar una ley y no guardarla exactamente, y es fementido quien desdize con la vida lo que professa con la religion" (ivi, pp. 358–59).
43 "Las vanderas de Cruz que avia en el exercito eran muchas y en los mismos reales entre las armas se oyan con gran fervor los sermones de nuestra santa Fe, y parecia en buena parte aquel exercito de Catolicos" (ivi, p. 363).
44 "Dixo despues Cubosama que mas valian mil soldados en manos de Iusto, que diez mil en las de qualquier capitan" (ivi, p. 365).
45 Guido Mongini, *Censura e identità nella prima storiografia gesuitica (1547–1572)*, in *Nunc alia tempora, alii mores. Storici e storia in età postridentina. Atti del Convegno internazionale, Torino, 24–27 settembre 2003*, ed. M. Firpo, Firenze, Olschki, 2005, pp. 179–88.
46 Pedro Morejòn, *Relacion de la persecucion que vuo en la yglesia de Japon: y de los insignes martyres, que gloriosamente dieron su vida en defensa de nostra santa Fè, el Año de 1614 y 1615*, en Mexico, por Ioan Ruyz, 1616, pp. 49–55, 98–103.
47 Morishita, *L'art des missions catholiques au Japon (XVIᵉ–XVIIᵉ siècle)*. Antonella Romano, *Un espacio tripolar de las misiones: Europa, Asia y América*, in Elisabetta Corsi (ed.), *Ordenes religiosas entre América y Asia: Ideas para una historia misionera de los espacios coloniales*, México, Colmex, 2008, pp. 253–77; Romano, *Impressions de Chine*, cit., pp. 261–87.
48 Hsia, *La Controriforma*, cit., pp. 202–4.
49 Pedro Morejón, *Relacion de la persecucion que huvo estos años contra la Iglesia de Iapon, y los ministros della*, en Caragoça, por Juan de Larumbe, 1617, pp. 61–69, 125–44; in the Roman archives of the Society there is also an Italian version of the biographical profile of Morejón known as *De laudibus Iusti*, in which the richer versions of the passages dedicated to Ukon are taken up (ARSI, Jap.Sin., 46, ff. 365–74).
50 Piñeiro, *Relacíon del suceso que tuvo nuestra santa fe en los Reinos del Japón*, cit., pp. 360, 362, 366.
51 On this point Piñeiro does the same: "Viendose Dario ya viejo, noquiso morir con el cargo de su estado, y fue tan cuerdo, que queriendo tener por suya sola la hora de su muerte, pues en las de la vida avian tenido tanta parte, los negocios, la guerra, el govierno del estado, y o tras cosas del mundo, que distraen y divierten el alma de su principal fin, supo escoger los ultimos dias de la vida, para retirado atender a solas, y en reposo con Dios, y en el, y con el hallar una muerte quieta, y tras ella la salvacion" (ivi, p. 358).
52 Tronu Montane, *Sacred Space and Ritual in Early Modern Japan*, cit., p. 105.
53 The testimony is reported in *Summarium documentorum*, in *Positio della causa di beatificazione di Justus Takayama Ukon*, pp. 558–65.
54 "rosto muy alegre et aprasivel [...] esperando que a Igreja romana nos declare por Martyr a quem tanto per ella soube padecer" (Antonio Fransico Cardim, *Elogios e ramalhete de flores borrifado com o sangue dos religiosos da Companhia de Iesu, a quem os tyrannos do Imperio de Iappaõ tiraraõ as vidas por odio da Fè Catholica*, em Lisboa, por Manoel da Sylva, 1650, pp. 249–59).
55 Francisco Colin, *Labor evangelica, ministerios apostolicos de los obreros de la Compania de Iesus, fundacion, y progressos de su. Provincia en las islas filipinas*, en Madrid, por Joseph Fernandez de Buendia, 1663, pp. 725–45.

56 Su Colin cf. Eduardo Descalzo Yuste, *La compañía de Jesús en Filipinas (1581–1768): realidad y representación*, PhD thesis, under the direction of José Luis Betrán Moya, Universidad Autónoma de Barcelona, Bellaterra, 2015, pp. 407–14.
57 Colin, *Labor evangelica*, cit., p. 725. Cf. also Roldán-Figueroa, *The Martyrs of Japan*, cit., pp. 188, 192–94.
58 It is Colin himself who provides an interesting indication of how Guzman's text was circulated in the Philippines: "Algunos y particularmente el señor governador tenian ya noticia por los libros del padre Luis de Guzman de su nobleza y grandes hazanas, y de los particulares servicios que avia hecho a la Iglesia del Iapon" (ivi, pp. 740–41).
59 "Fue tambien general el consuelo, y satisfacion que todos sentian en sus almas, como en muerte de un varon Santo, y justo, persuadiendose, no era ageno de la Corona de Martyr, pues fue causada claramente de las incomodidades del destierro" (ivi, p. 744); see also pp. 742–43.
60 Ivi, p. 736.
61 Ivi, p. 739.
62 "largas horas [...] la cosas del Iapon [...] Don Iusto siempre se Avia criado en la Corte, y avia manejado las majores materias de estado, en paz, y Guerra, y tenia tan gran juizio, llenava con sus repuestas tan acertadamente las preguntas del Governador, que cada dia se iba aficionando mas" (ivi, p. 742).
63 "varon santo [...] besarle lo spies, como a Santo Martir" (ivi, p. 744).
64 "los mismos religiosos, causando en los Iapones admiracion, y edificacion muy grande [...] separar los huessos de tan ilustre varon, y martyr de Christo de los demas, y ponerlos en un caxon bien adornado en la Capilla interior del Colegio, con un retrato suyo de pincel encima" (ivi, p. 745).
65 Roldán-Figueroa, *The Martyrs of Japan*, cit., p. 208.
66 On the role of hagiographies as tools for mobilizing a cultic memory and for building profiles of holiness cf. Simon Ditchfield, *"Historia magistra sanctitatis"? The relationship betwen historiography in Italy after the Council of Trent (1564–1742ca.)*, in *Nunc alia tempora, alii mores. Storici e storia in età postridentina*, cit., pp. 16–18.
67 "Antes que lo enterrassen fue puesto su cuerpo en una sala muy bien adereçada, conlos mas lustrosos vestidos que usava: el rostro descubierto, al uso de Iapon, donde no se podia dar vado a la gente que acudia a verle, y besarle los pies, como a santo martir. Començo a besarle la mano el comissario del santo oficio" (Piñeiro, *Relacíon del suceso que tuvo nuestra santa fe en los Reinos del Japón*, cit., p. 350).
68 This is what Morejón reported in his deposition before the apostolic judges charged with collecting material for the cause of beatification of the Japanese martyrs: "Todos juntos con los restantes de a çiudad le acompañaron, reverençiandole como a sancto confessor de Christo, y como a tal le besaron las manos y tomaron algunas de sus cossas para reliquias, hasta que fue enterrado en el collegio de la Compañía de Jésus desta dicha çiudad" (*Summarium documentorum*, in *Positio della causa di beatificazione di Justus Takayama Ukon*, cit., p. 565).
69 Elena Bonora, *La Controriforma*, Roma-Bari, Laterza, 2001, pp. 98–100.
70 Gotor, *I beati del papa*, cit., pp. 308–19; Id., *Chiesa e santità nell'Italia moderna*, cit., pp. 85–87.
71 Ivi, pp. 108–10, 122–23.
72 Gotor, *I beati del papa*, cit., pp. 231–42; see also Imbruglia, *The Jesuit Missions of Paraguay and a Cultural History of Utopia (1568–1789)*, cit., pp. 111–12.
73 Omata Rappo, *Des Indes lointaines aux scènes des collèges*, cit., pp. 434, 448; similar is the approach of the eighteenth-century Jesuit historian Pierre François-Xavier de Charlevoix, who speaks of him as a "héros chrétien," "illustre encore

par ses vertus et par ses souffrances" (*Histoire de l'établissement, des progrès et de la décadence du Christianisme dans l'empire du Japon*, à Rouen, chez Jacques Joseph Le Boullenger, 1715, vol. 1, p. 233).
74 Roldán-Figueroa, *The Martyrs of Japan*, cit., pp. 261–62.
75 Pizzorusso, *Il martirio in odium fidei dalla realtà missionaria alla burocrazia romana*, cit., pp. 205–6.
76 The text is barely quoted in *Summarium testium*, p. 615.
77 Anton Witwer, *Informatio*, in *Positio della causa di beatificazione di Justus Takayama Ukon*, cit., p. 24.
78 martirio formale," "martirio materiale," "il martirio interiormente" (Ivi, p. 46).
79 "martirio superiore [...] significa provocare la morte violenta, quasi come colui che fa Harakiri, pensando che esso sia il frutto della sola decisione umana [...] dalla errata fiducia nelle proprie capacità" (Ivi, p. 67).
80 "differenza tra l'attivo desiderio del martirio e l'essere passivamente esposto a condizioni che solo lentamente conducono alla morte," "all'impotenza del Signore inchiodato alla croce" (ivi, p. 71).
81 "prendere dal fascino del potere, della gloria e del denaro" (Francis Xavier Mizobe Osamu, *Introductio generalis*, in *Positio della causa di beatificazione di Justus Takayama Ukon*, cit., p. 16).
82 *Summarium testium*, in *Positio della causa di beatificazione di Justus Takayama Ukon*, cit., pp. 141–42.

# Index nominum

Note: Page numbers followed by "n" denote endnotes.

Abraham 4, 15, 60n9, 65, 85, 91
Acquaviva, C. 21n18, 21n23, 42n34, 43n43, 77n15
Adam 48
Alexander the Great 92
Almeida, L. de 42n39
Alonge, G. 46n94, 60n6
Alonge Guarnieri, Z. v
Alonso Romo, E. J. 98n5
Alvarez-Taladriz, J. L. 9n28
Amakusa, G. 25
Amakusa, S. (Miguel) 24, 25
Amato, A. 81
Amsler, N. 22n28
Andreu, F. 78n35
Antaeus 79n43
Araki, M. 85, 91
Aranha, P. 8n11, 9n23
Ardissino, E. 78n35, 79n39, 79n42, 79n43
Aresi, P. 72, 73, 75, 78n36, 78n38, 79n41, 79n43, 79n44, 79n48
Arima, H. (Protasius) 50, 53, 54, 61n24
Augustine of Hippo 12
Azria, R. 8n11

Badea, A. 22n28
Balz, H. 60n9
Balzamo, N. 62n34, 64n78, 64n81
Bartoli, D. 12, 20n8, 20n9, 22n29, 24, 26, 27, 28, 34, 40n5, 41n15, 41n17, 41n19, 41n22, 41n27, 41n29, 43n54, 44n56, 44n57, 44n66, 44n67, 45n78, 61n22, 62n34, 64n76, 77n11
Bellarmino, R. 94

Berry, M. E. 21n15
Betrán Moya, J. L. 102n56
Bonora, E. ix, 102n69
Borromeo, C. 72
Boscaro, A. 40n2
Botero, G. 40n11, 43n52, 99n25
Bourdon, L. 43n55
Bowersock, G. W. 76n2
Boxer, C. R., 21n11, 61n24, 61n28
Bozzola, S. 61n21
Broggio, P. 78n30
Brown, P. 62n30, 62n32
Buddha 34, 56
Busi, G. 60n5, 63n67

Cabral, F. 9n24, 14, 24, 51
Camaioni, M. 46n94
Canisio, P. 94
Carandini, S. 78n30
Cardim, A. F. 92, 101n54
Carletti, F. 65, 77n6
Carrión, F. 85
Carvalho, G. 22n27, 40n7, 42n34, 45n75, 60n12, 79n40
Casale, V. 78n30
Castel-Branco, C. 22n27, 40n7, 42n34, 45n75, 60n12, 79n40
Castro, X. de 8n5
Catharina 26
Catherine de' Medici 38
Catto, M. 8n12, 61n27, 99n28
Cerqueira, L. 68
Charlevoix, P.-F.-X. de 62n34, 102n73
Christin, O. 45n76, 45n91, 60n6, 62n34, 64n78, 64n80, 64n81
Coelho, G. 13
Colin, F. 92, 93, 94, 101n55, 102n56, 102n57, 102n58

## Index nominum

Colombo, E. 78n33, 78n34, 79n50
Cooper, M. 98n12
Corsi, E. 101n47
Couros, M. de 86, 88, 99n30

Descalzo Yuste, E. 102n56
Di Russo, M. 9n23
Diefendorf, B. B. 45n87, 45n92
Ditchfield, S. 78n29, 78n32, 78n33, 102n66

Ehrman, B. D. 60n9, 60n11, 62n31
Eliade, M. 41n14, 45n86, 46n96, 60n4, 60n10, 61n19, 63n55
Elison, G. 61n24
Elisonas, J. 8n6, 21n21
Eve 48

Fabian 57, 58
Fabietti, U. 8n9, 61n17, 62n47, 97n2
Fabre, P. A. ix, 8n11, 8n12, 9n17, 9n20, 79n51, 80n53
Fagiolo Dell'Arco, Marcello 78n30
Felici, L. ix
Felipe de Jesús (de las Casas) 70
Filoramo, G. 46n97
Fiorani, L. 78n30
Firpo, M. ix, 10n32, 46n94, 101n45
Flückiger, F. 62n34, 64n78, 64n80, 64n81
Francis of Assisi, saint 38, 66, 67
Fraser, R. 61n19
Frazer, J. G. 61n19
Frei, E. 20n8
Froís, L. 40n4, 41n21, 42n42, 44n61, 44n63, 48, 52, 53, 54, 55, 56, 60n12, 62n35, 62n49, 66, 67, 68, 73, 77n7, 77n16, 79n40, 85, 98n13
Fulvio, G. 21n23

Gago, B. 30, 33
García Bernal, J. J. 78n30
Gay, J.-P. 79n49
Ghermani, N. 64n80
Gnecchi Soldo, O. 5, 8n15, 10n29, 27, 28, 32, 42n31, 42n34, 68, 83
Gomez, P. 53
Gonzáles-Bolado, J. 40n4
Gotor, M. 78n31, 78n32, 97n1, 98n4, 98n6, 102n70, 102n72
Granada, L. de 20n5
Grassi, U. 20n8

Greenblatt, S. 60n6
Gruzinsky, S. 8n3, 8n4
Guarnieri, F. R. ix
Guasti, N. 20n1
Gumppenberg, W. 59, 64n72
Guzmán, L. de 78n37, 92, 99n24, 102n58

Hall, J. W. 8
Hannibal 92
Hercules 79n43
Hervieu-Leger, D. 8n11
Hesselink, R. H. 22n27, 76n5
Heyberger, B. 22n28
Hsia, R. P-C. 9n18, 9n21, 78n32, 101n48

Ignatius of Loyola 2, 6, 11, 34, 49, 66, 71, 75, 78n33
Ikegami, E. 7n2
Imbruglia, G. 10n29, 20n1, 22n33, 76n2, 77n10, 79n51, 102n72
Isgrò, G. 61n20, 62n33
Ishida, M. 15

Jacob, saint 45n82
Jesus (Christ) 2, 3, 6, 13, 18, 25, 26, 28, 32, 33, 34, 35, 36, 39, 45n82, 48, 53, 54, 55, 60n9, 65, 73, 89, 93, 95, 97, 98n21, 99n29, 100n41, 102n68
Jiménez Pablo, E. 8n11, 98n5
João 25
Job 86, 96
Jones, L. 60n4
Juan de Santa María 66, 77n8, 77n12, 77n14
Julia, D. 64n79

Konishi, Y. (Agostinho) 15, 21n23, 50–51, 84
Kouamé, N. 9n22, 20n4, 41n21, 44n58, 46n95
Krumenacker, Y. 45n76

Lage Reis Correia, P. 9n24, 21n12, 77n13
Lancillotto, N. 40n12
Laures, J. 21n19
Lavenia, V. 9n24
Leão 52
Lévi-Strauss, C. 4–5, 8n14, 48
Lourenço 83
Luczkiw, S. xi

Luther, M. 2
Luzzatto, S. 97n2

Maeda, family 86
Maeda, T. 84, 93
Maffei, G. P. 98n8
Martin, saint 52
Martínez Millán, J. 8n11, 98n5
Mary (Virgin) 3, 28, 33, 35, 37, 38, 41n31, 44n63, 52, 59, 60
Mathias 55
Mercurian, E. 8n15, 42n31
Michael the Archangel, saint 28, 41n31
Miguel 52, 53
Mizobe, F. S. O. 103n81
Mongini, G. 8n12, 20n1, 20n5, 43n53, 75, 76n4, 79n50, 79n51, 80n52, 101n45
Morejón, P. 36, 82, 90, 91, 94, 98n5, 99n27, 101n46, 101n49, 102n68
Morishita, S. 23n35, 44n71, 60n2, 61n29, 101n47
Mostaccio, S. 8n12

Nakamura, K. M. 61n13, 61n15, 61n18, 63n56
Naohiro, A. 21n14
Neri, F. 71
Ninomiya, H. 21n13, 40n1, 61n25
Nobili, R. de' 5

Ochino, B. 39
Oda, family 50, 85, 91
Oda, N. 14, 27, 36, 50, 83, 85, 89, 91, 100n40
Omata Rappo, H. 9n19, 23n34, 44n62, 63n70, 64n76, 77n20, 77n27, 78n30, 98n5, 102n73
Ōmura, Y. (Sancho) 55
Ota Mishima, M. E. 23n35
Ōtomo, S. 15, 21n24
Ōtomo, Y. (Sōrin) 15

Pastore, S. 9n24
Paul of Tarsus, saint 48, 68, 77n18
Paulo 36
Paulo (Fabian's son) 57
Pavone, S. 9n24
Peltier, J. 21n22
Peter, saint 96
Petrolini, C. 9n24

Index nominum    107

Petrucci, M. G. 21n20
Philip II Habsburg 66
Pierre, B. 8n11, 8n12
Piñeiro, L. 35, 44n72, 58, 64n77, 88, 89, 91, 93, 94, 96, 98n3, 99n32, 101n50, 101n51, 102n67
Pizarro Llorente, H. 8n11, 98n5
Pizzorusso, G. 10n30, 23n33, 76n3, 78n32, 80n54, 103n75
Polo, M. 2, 8n7
Prenestino, A. 21n18
Prosperi, A. 9n16, 9n24, 20n8, 45n85, 76n1, 78n30
Proust, J. 7n1, 8n16, 20n6, 62n45
Prudhomme, C. 46n95

Quadros, A. de 42n39
Quiles García, F. 78n30

Rai, E. 79n52
Rambelli, F. 61n14, 63n63
Raviola, B. A. 99n25
Raynaud, T. 75
Ribadeneira, P. de 95
Ricci, M. 5
Ries, J. 46n96, 60n4, 60n7
Rodriguez Giram, J. 57, 68
Roldán-Figueroa, R. 64n77, 77n8, 77n9, 77n21, 77n24, 78n37, 99n24, 102n57, 102n65, 103n74
Romano, A. 8n8, 9n18, 77n23, 101n47
Roscioni, G. C. 22n33, 76n1
Rose of Lima 90
Ruiz de Medina, J. 40n7, 40n12, 99n31
Rurale, F. 9n17

Sanfilippo, M. 9n24
Schneider, G. 60n9
Schurhammer, G. 40n10, 44n64
Schütte, J. F. 45n83, 61n27
Seidel Menchi, S. 45n76
Sen-no-Rikyū 84
Shimazu, T. 26
Shōmu, emperor 56
Silva, J. de 100n35
Simão 55
Spineto, N. ix, 40n8
Stark, R. 8n10, 20n7
Steichen, M. 21n16, 40n4, 61n24
Subrahmanyam, S. 8n5
Sullivan, L. E. 61n13

Takayama, family 83, 84
Takayama, U. (Justus) 5, 6, 14, 15, 35, 36, 51, 76, 81–103
Takayama, Z. (Dario) 36, 82, 91, 98n8, 101n51
Takizawa, O. 20n2, 22n26
Tamburello, A. 9n23
Tanzio da Varallo (Antonio d'Enrico) 74, 79n47
Teresa of Avila 72
Tertullian, Q. S. F. 18, 73
Tokugawa, family 27, 36, 72, 91
Tokugawa, I. 15, 45n83, 57, 88
Tommaso 44n66
Toyotomi, family 15
Toyotomi, H(ideyori) 93
Toyotomi, H(ideyoshi) 13, 14, 15, 17, 18, 30, 35, 36, 39, 50, 51, 66, 67, 77n14, 84, 85, 87, 89, 90, 91, 93, 100n40, 101n42
Trento, M. 9n17, 9n27
Trigault, N. 64n76
Tripepi, A. 23n36
Tronu Montane, C. 8n11, 22n27, 22n28, 22n30, 40n9, 43n46, 60n1, 76n5, 101n52

Ucerler, M. A. J. 8n11, 9n23, 10n31, 20n2, 43n51, 62n32, 98n7, 98n11
Urban VIII Barberini 70, 71

Vacchini da Viterbo, F. 82
Valignano, A. 5, 6, 9n24, 9n28, 10n29, 17, 20, 22n31, 24, 28, 31, 32, 43n43, 43n47, 51, 52, 55, 61n24, 61n27, 67, 77n9, 77n15, 83, 87, 88, 95, 98n9
Vauchez, A. 64n79
Vesco, S. 60n2
Vilela, G. 32, 33, 83
Villani, P. 61n13
Villari, R. 9n16
Vittori, R. 82
Vu Thanh, H. 8n13, 9n22, 9n23, 9n26, 20n2, 20n5, 20n6, 22n30, 40n4, 41n16, 76n5, 77n11, 77n19

Ward, H. N. 22n32, 41n16
Wickham, C. 62n30
Wicki, J. 40n4, 40n10, 44n64
Windler, C. 22n28
Wipszycka, E. 62n30
Witwer, A. 45n73, 103n77

Xavier, F. 6, 11, 24, 25, 34, 35, 40n10, 44n60, 44n64, 48, 61n20, 66, 72, 78n33, 83, 96

Zorzi, A. 8n7
Županov, I. G. 8n11, 9n17, 20n3

For Product Safety Concerns and Information please contact our EU representative  GPSR@taylorandfrancis.com
Taylor & Francis Verlag GmbH, Kaufingerstraße 24, 80331 München, Germany

www.ingramcontent.com/pod-product-compliance
Lightning Source LLC
Chambersburg PA
CBHW051755230426
43670CB00012B/2298